W9-BCQ-567

DATE DUE
191168

The Black Bard *of* North Carolina

CHAPEL HILL BOOKS

The Black Bard *of* North Carolina

George Moses Horton *and His Poetry*

EDITED BY *Joan R. Sherman*

The University of North Carolina Press *Chapel Hill & London*

Set in Minion type by Eric M. Brooks
Design by Richard Hendel
Manufactured in the
United States of America
The paper in this book meets the
guidelines for permanence and
durability of the Committee on
Production Guidelines for Book
Longevity of the Council on
Library Resources.
Library of Congress
Cataloging-in-Publication Data
Horton, George Moses, 1798?–ca. 1880.
The Black bard of North Carolina:
George Moses Horton and His Poetry /
edited by Joan R. Sherman.
p. cm.
"Chapel Hill books."
"Works by George Moses Horton": p.
Includes bibliographical references and
index.
ISBN 0-8078-2341-4 (cloth: alk. paper).—
ISBN 0-8078-4648-1 (pbk.: alk. paper)
1. Afro-Americans—North Carolina—
Poetry. 2. Slavery—North Carolina—
Poetry. 3. Slaves—North Carolina—
Poetry. I. Sherman, Joan R. II. Title.
PS1999.H473A6 1997
811'.4—dc21 96-39347
CIP

01 00 99 98 97 5 4 3 2 1

CONTENTS

Introduction, 1

History, 1

Criticism, 32

Editorial Note, 44

Bibliography, 47

Works by George Moses Horton, 47

Reference Works, 48

UNCOLLECTED POEMS, 53

POEMS FROM *The Hope of Liberty*, 71

POEMS FROM *The Poetical Works*, 93

POEMS FROM *Naked Genius*, 119

Index of Titles, 157

ILLUSTRATIONS

Letter to Horace Greeley, 24

Pages one and eight of "An Address," 26–27

"The Poet's Feeble Petition," 63

"For the fair Miss M. M. McL[ean]
An acrostic [MARY MCLEAN]," 65

"The Emigrant Girl," 66–67

"An acrostic on the pleasures of beauty [JULIA SHEPARD]," 68

"An acrostic by George Horton [LUCY G. WRIGHT]"
and "An acrostic by George Horton the negro bard
[JANE E. MCIVER]," 69

Title page of *The Hope of Liberty*, 70

Title page of *Naked Genius*, 120

The Black Bard *of* North Carolina

Introduction

HISTORY

George Moses Horton was a slave for sixty-eight years, from his birth in about 1797 until the close of the Civil War. His achievements as a man and a poet were extraordinary: Horton was the first American slave to protest his bondage in verse; the first African American to publish a book in the South; the only slave to earn a significant income by selling his poems; the only poet of any race to produce a book of poems *before* he could write; and the only slave to publish two volumes of poetry while in bondage and another shortly after emancipation. Horton also stands out among African American poets of the nineteenth century for his wide range of poetical subjects and unorthodox attitudes. His religious verse is undogmatic and humanistic; his antislavery poems are honest and deeply personal, unlike the generic protests by free black poets; he treats everyday matters like drinking and poverty, women, love, and marriage with wry and cynical humor in an often self-satirical mood; and his view of America and its heroes is patriotic, integrationist, and culturally nationalistic. Above all, Horton's unbounded enthusiasm for liberty, nature, and his sacred art of poetry vitalizes his best poems, and we hear a real, self-aware individual speaking directly to us.

At a time when the life expectancy for a white male was about thirty-five years and much less for a slave, George Horton survived to the age of eighty-six. Unfortunately, the only sources of concrete information about his long life as a slave and free man are his autobiographical sketch in *The Poetical Works* (1845), a few of his letters, one long oration, and brief reminiscences by men who actually met him.

Horton was born in Northampton County, four miles from the Roanoke River on the small tobacco farm of his master, William Horton. He says in *The Poetical Works* that he was the sixth of ten children and that his mother had five girls, "not of one father," followed by George, another boy, and three more girls "by her second husband."[1] A few years after George's birth, his master decided to move from Northampton County because of "the sterility of his land" to Chatham County, some 100 miles southwest, where he purchased land in 1800.

William Horton's household in this year consisted of five female relatives, plus one of his six sons (five others had left the farm), and eight slaves, including George, George's mother, her five girls, and one other slave. William Horton soon sold his Northampton farm and settled his household in Chatham, nine miles from Pittsborough on high lands between the Haw River and New Hope Creek. In the next few years, he bought more land and by 1806 owned more than 400 acres, planted mainly in corn and wheat. On this prosperous farm, George was a "cow-boy" for ten years, an occupation he found "disagreeable." His life's pleasures, he writes, were "singing lively tunes" and "hearing people read," and with his brother, "both remarkable for boys of color and hard raising," George resolved to learn to read. He learned the alphabet from "old parts" of tattered spelling books and studied the words outdoors every Sabbath and indoors at night by "incompetent bark of brush light, almost exhausted by the heat of the fire, and almost suffocated with smoke." His "scheme" to learn spelling and reading was "repeatedly threatened" by local "play boys" who taunted him for his foolish studying and by his master who cared little for his own children's schooling and "less for the improvement of the mind of his servants." But, Horton says, he persevered "with an indefatigable resolution" and "with defiance." The obstacles he had to overcome, Horton concludes, "had an auspicious tendency to waft me, as on pacific gales, above the storms of envy and the calumniating scourge of emulation, from which literary imagination often sinks beneath its dignity, and instruction languishes at the shrine of vanity." Horton developed this extraordinary vocabulary by reading "parts of the New Testament," his mother's Wesley hymnal, "other pieces of poetry from various authors," and, later on, many books. To these texts he added the tunes and rhythms of religious music that he heard at Sabbath preachings and camp meetings, and he soon "composed several undigested pieces" on religious themes in his head, such as "Excited from Reading the Obedience of Nature to Her Lord in the Vessel on the Sea."

William Horton was seventy-seven years old in 1814 when he decided to "confer part of his servants on his children, lots were cast, and his son James fell heir to me," wrote George. He was about seventeen and now worked in the fields alongside James Horton's sons on the Chatham farm. When George looked back on this farm labor in his "Address" of 1859, he referred to himself as "a plough broken receptacle" and urged students to cultivate their talents as he could never do, "confined to a horse and tottering plough."[2] William Horton died in 1819, and a few years later, when his estate was distributed among the family, James bought three of his father's twelve slaves, Judy, Lucy, and Ben. George Horton evokes the memory of this event in his poems "Division of an Estate," "A Slave's Reflection on the Eve Before His Sale," and "Farewell to Frances."

Aside from his dislike of manual labor and his sadness over the breaking up and dispersal of the estate's slaves Horton revealed few details about his slavery years in his writings. But it seems certain that his bondage was relatively mild, since he enjoyed much freedom of movement beginning in about 1817. Horton used Saturday afternoon and all day Sunday, the slave's traditional time off, to walk eight miles to Chapel Hill, where he sold fruit and his poems. Beginning in the 1830s, the poet hired his time and lived in Chapel Hill, away from his master's farm. Horton no doubt benefited from the attitudes and laws of North Carolina, which in the first three decades of the century were markedly more liberal toward slaves than those of other southern states. Many North Carolinians, their public officials, and newspapers freely and actively advocated emancipation of the slaves, and they supported national antislavery organizations such as the National Convention for the Abolition of Slavery and the American Colonization Society. Colonization, which aimed to resettle freed slaves in Liberia, Haiti, and elsewhere, was an active movement nationwide between 1816 and 1832. In 1816, the North Carolina legislature requested Congress to establish a colony for emancipated slaves on the Pacific coast, and in 1819 an agent of the American Colonization Society organized a regional chapter in Raleigh; ten additional North Carolina chapters formed in the next ten years.[3]

Despite free expression of antislavery views in North Carolina, little practical action was taken to free the slaves, except by the Quakers. Since 1768, North Carolina Quakers had propagandized against the slave trade and for emancipation; they illegally freed slaves they owned or transferred their legal titles to the Society of Friends; they appointed agents to accept title to slaves from non-Quaker masters who wished to free them; and they repeatedly petitioned the North Carolina General Assembly to abolish slavery. In 1816, Quakers founded the North Carolina Manumission Society, which worked to liberalize slave laws, emancipate slaves, and then educate them.[4] North Carolina Quakers also originated the Underground Railroad, the organization that expanded nationwide to help runaway slaves reach border states, the North, and Canada until the Civil War. This system of safe houses and transportation for fugitives began in 1819 in North Carolina, when Levi Coffin and his cousin, Vestal, set up the first station of the Railroad at their home near New Garden in Guilford County.[5]

North Carolina's relatively liberal laws granted many of the same legal protections to slaves as to freemen, and during the 1820s, the North Carolina legislature rejected several efforts of proslavery interests to restrict activities of slaves and of emancipation societies. The state's antislavery sentiments and organizations and its milder laws derived in part from the unique qualities of slaveholdings in North Carolina. Although the state's slave population had been rising steadily from 1790, by 1830 the number of slaves and slaveholding families remained low relative to those in neighboring Virginia and South Carolina; moreover, North Carolinians held fewer slaves per family. Of the 14,973 North Carolina slaveholding families in 1830, almost 95 percent held fewer than 20 slaves, and 85 percent of these owned just 1 to 9 slaves.[6] The few wealthy tobacco and cotton plantations with large slaveholdings were concentrated in the Roanoke River Valley on or near the Virginia border. Here, slavery was as harsh as in the rest of the South, but slavery elsewhere in North Carolina was milder, more patriarchal because the farms were small and required few slaves, much like the ones on which George Horton grew up and labored.

North Carolina's slavery was milder also because the state's population was preponderantly white; and with the few large groups of slaves isolated from one another on remote plantations, the state experienced far fewer slave revolts than did its southern neighbors. Only five uprisings occurred in North Carolina during the entire eighteenth century, and nine between 1800 and 1829. Among these were rebellions in May and June of 1802 throughout a dozen North Carolina counties, which resulted in the arrest and torture of hundreds of slaves and execution of twenty-four. In 1805, slaves in three counties conspired to poison their masters—and they succeeded in several instances— before twenty of them were arrested, tortured and lashed, and four were killed. A planned revolt of North Carolina and Virginia slaves was discovered in 1810; and in 1821, a month-long dangerous rebellion of maroons (outlawed fugitive slaves), aided by free blacks, required the militia of three North Carolina counties to suppress it. North Carolinians' fears of slave revolts were reinforced by numerous serious uprisings outside the state, with those of Gabriel Prosser in Virginia (1800) and Denmark Vesey in South Carolina (1822) arousing the greatest alarm. The Gabriel Plot, which probably involved many thousands of slaves in Richmond and several Virginia counties, had direct repercussions in North Carolina, where twenty-one suspected followers of Gabriel were hanged and many others whipped and deported. Although we have no evidence that such slave revolts directly impinged upon Horton's life, they did alter the liberal climate in North Carolina, especially after 1830, thus contributing perhaps to the failure of Horton's several attempts to secure his freedom.

By 1820, Horton's routine of weekly Sabbath walks to Chapel Hill was well established, and he had launched a career as a professional poet on the campus of the state university. The University of North Carolina had been born with George Horton in the last decade of the eighteenth century: it was chartered by the legislature in 1789 and opened its doors to students in 1795, the first university in the South to do so. The site of New Hope Chapel had been chosen for "the purity of the water, the salubrity of the air and the great healthfulness of the climate" as well as its geographic location in the center of the state, at the intersection of two major roads.[7] The first term began with forty-one students, rising to one hundred in the second term, with a faculty of five that included a professor of Humanity at its head. In 1804 the trustees elected as president Joseph Caldwell, who from the 1820s until his death in 1835 befriended the campus poet, George Horton. Caldwell, a fine teacher and administrator, won praise for his scholarship, eloquence, and tireless, skillful dedication to the university. He energetically defended UNC against its early foes and its continual financial problems. Because the university's founding charter made no provision for state financial support, the school depended on private and public donations of money and land; but North Carolinians did not give these generously, feeling that the university was too expensive, too difficult to reach from all areas of the state, and that its liberal and skeptical teachings were insufficiently Christian. Lack of support for the university was typical of the backwardness in education (and in industry, agriculture, commerce, transportation, banking, the arts, and democratic government) that characterized North Carolina, the "Rip Van Winkle State," during the first three decades of the century. North Carolinians at that time were known as conservative, individualistic, provincial, apathetic, and resistant to change; and the state ranked very low among states of the Union.

The university that George Horton frequented in the early 1820s was far from prosperous, and the financial panic of 1825 so aggravated its economic and physical decline that "by 1830 the University seemed on the verge of ruin."[8] The Chapel Hill campus had never been beautiful, except for its abundant trees; it stood a poor relation to the University of Virginia, founded in 1819 by Thomas Jefferson, who designed its splendid neoclassical buildings and elegant lawns. In contrast, the North Carolina campus consisted of two plain brick buildings, named East and South, tiny Person Hall, Steward's Hall, which was "an ugly two-storied wooden structure," the simple president's house, and a grammar school.[9] In his account of his life up to 1830, Horton revealed the experiences on campus that greatly mattered to him. On one hand, he disapproved of the collegians' pranks, their putting the slave on display, and their drinking; on the other hand, he celebrated his verse-making and reading, his manumission campaign, and publication of his *Hope of Liberty* in 1829. The sketchy facts about campus life that Horton's autobiography supplies are supported by historians' accounts of the university during these early decades and afterward.

Chapel Hill students, the sons of wealthy planters, seemed more interested in sports, gambling, and pleasures of the table than in their studies. They often engaged in boisterous riots and at various times destroyed laboratories, recitation rooms, and blackboards. They attacked faculty with clubs, stones, and pistols; sang ribald songs; violently rang the university bell; painted a professor's horse; stole farmers' produce and animals; and perpetrated assorted vulgar and dangerous pranks.[10] The collegians, Horton wrote, "for their diversion were fond of pranking with the country servants," and they "pranked" with him by insisting that he "spout"; they made him "stand forth and address" the collegians extemporaneously, "as an orator of inspired promptitude." Public speaking and debate were strongly encouraged at the university: all seniors delivered orations in May, men awarded honors gave commencement speeches, and all students were required to join one of the "oratory" societies, the Dialectic or the Philosophic. Since "the oration was the highest type of literary effort developed in the ante-bellum South,"[11] it was fitting that students transformed Horton into an orator. At first, the slave felt proud of his performance, he wrote; "but I soon found it an object of aversion, and considered myself nothing but a public ignoramus." Consequently Horton abandoned these "foolish harangues and began to speak of poetry." On two known later occasions, however, he again "spouted" to order for the collegians, and in his "Address" he called himself "your sable orator" and "your poor orator."

George Horton was not the only black servant who catered to UNC students' whims. Richard Benbury Creecy, an 1835 graduate of the university, wrote about Dave Barum, a sensible and practical, "faithful college servant, a great favorite with the boys" who was a "bitter and jealous" rival of Horton's at the university.[12] Kemp Plummer Battle, an 1849 graduate of Carolina, tutor, professor, and later university president, also recalled "Dave Barham" [sic] and November Caldwell as the two full-time slave servants living on the campus. Battle remembered several other "negroes, who in different ways contributed to the amusement and comfort of students," including "licensed wood-cutters"; the Merritt brothers, "who owned opossum dogs" and guided students on night hunts for raccoons and possums; and Sam Morphis, a mulatto slave who hired his time to drive "hacks." Battle noted two other black servants who gave demeaning performances like Horton's: Ben Boothe's talent was to split open planks of wood on his head (at a charge of five cents each), and "Yatney" realistically imitated a dog fight.[13]

By all accounts, university students, faculty, and servants drank steadily and heavily, and George Horton joined them. The students, he wrote, flattered him "into the belief that it [drinking] would hang me on the wings of new inspiration, which would waft me into the regions of poetical perfection." Excessive drinking had plagued Horton since his teenage years, he recalled, when he "was raised in a family or neighborhood inclined to dissipation," and William Horton often gave his laborers "the ordinary dram, of which he was much too fond himself." Following the master's example, the slaves "partook freely in order to brave the storms of hardship, and thought it an honor to be intoxicated." In those days, Horton said, when "Bacchus was honored far more than Ceres," "libertinism, obscenity and profanation were in their full career." Men distilled whiskey and drank even on the Sabbath. Horton, looking back, lamented his "misfortune to become a votary of that growing evil." The evil of drink was so pervasive at the university that in 1829 students formed a Temperance Society, and an 1837 ordinance made it a dismissible offense to bring "intoxicating liquor" into college buildings. A later code (1855) prohibited all houses within two miles of Chapel Hill that sold any quantity "of spirituous, vinous, or malt liquors" and forbade anyone to sell or give away spirits that would be used within two miles of the campus. Clearly these measures did not work, for at the 1859 commencement, President James Buchanan condemned intemperance, and in the same year a Committee of Examiners report criticized students' "use of intoxicating liquors."[14] George Horton, however, claimed in 1845 that he had outgrown his habit. He had discovered "the moral evil of excessive drinking," penitentially rejected the allure of "the music of sirens," and embraced "the beneficial effects of temperance and regularity." Horton commented on his struggles with alcohol and warned of the evils of drink in poems like "The Tippler to His Bottle" and "The Intemperance Club" and in his "Address."

When Horton ceased orating on command for the students, he began "the experiment of acrostics" and became part-time poet-in-residence at Chapel Hill. During the week, "at the handle of the plow" he composed poems to order in his head—he could not write until about 1832—and dictated them to student buyers on the next Sabbath. Horton recalled selling "love pieces in verse . . . and acrostics on the names of many of the tip-top belles of Virginia, South Carolina, and Georgia" for the princely sums of twenty-five to seventy-five cents each, "besides many decent and respectable suits of clothes." Students who knew him in Chapel Hill tallied the flourishing sales of his love poems and acrostics. Richard Creecy wrote that Horton's weekly "average budget of lyrics was about a dozen in number. . . . We usually invested a quarter a week, and generally to the tune of the girl we left behind us."[15] Kemp Battle reported that Horton's "love-letters were quite eloquent" and often effective and that he wrote "for the students acrostics on the names of their sweethearts. When his employer was willing to pay fifty cents the poem was generously gushing. Twenty-five cents procured one more lukewarm in passion."[16] Horton's clients also supplied their poet with books; he names twenty-two donors of books in his memoir. Among the books Horton lists were "Murray's English Grammar . . . Johnson's Dictionary" and other dictionaries, "Milton's Paradise Lost, Thomson's Seasons, parts of Homer's Iliad and Vergil's Aeneid, Beauties of Shakespeare, Beauties of Byron, part of Plutarch, Morse's Geography, the Columbian Orator, Snowden's History of the Revolution, [and] Young's Night Thoughts." From this library Horton culled poetic forms and subjects and a vocabulary laden with mythological, literary, and historical allusions.

Chapel Hill's poet had been versifying for almost ten years when he encountered a woman who put his verse into print. "To the much distinguished Mrs. Hentz," Horton wrote, "I owe much for the correction of many poetical errors. Being a professional poetess herself and a lover of genius, she discovered my little uncultivated talent. . . ." His benefactress inspired and edited Horton's art and wrote down verses he dictated. Even more, Horton recalled, Mrs. Hentz was "unequivocally anxious to announce the birth of my recent and astonishing fame, and sent its blast on the gale of passage back to the frozen plains of Massachusetts." Horton's muse and patron, Caroline Lee Whiting Hentz (1800–1856) of Lancaster, Massachusetts, had accompanied her husband, Nicholas Marcellus Hentz (1797–1856), to the University of North Carolina in 1826, where he was professor of modern languages until 1831. The Hentzs subsequently worked as educators in half a dozen states, while Mrs. Hentz raised four children and became a popular, prolific author of poems, plays, and dozens of romantic novels and story collections.

In many of her works, Mrs. Hentz expressed affection for the South and strong religious sentiments that perhaps motivated her kindness to Horton; but ironically, she was an apologist for slavery. Hentz's remembrance of George Horton appears in her novel, *Lovell's Folly* (1833); here she writes, in her own voice, that slaveholding inevitably fulfills the commandment "that the crimes of the fathers should be visited upon the children, . . . As well might we reproach the sable African for the color which severs him from our race, as the descendant of the southern planter for being *born* the hereditary owner of a race of slaves." Although she would never personally hold slaves, she would never deny her affections to the fated slaveholders. The second prong of Hentz's apologia is the happy condition of most slaves. Many "unhappy and degraded" slaves suffer brutal punishment and privations, she writes, but "there are many others who are mildly superintended by tender and benevolent masters, all their wants liberally supplied, and their wishes kindly indulged." Thus, she concludes, slavery is "sweetened," it does not injure the soul, and besides, the evil is "gradually disappearing" as emancipated slaves settle in Liberia (77–78). Mrs. Hentz's rose-colored view of the evil that would not disappear for another thirty-two years is reinforced in *Lovell's Folly* in the portrait of the heroine's grandfather, "owner of a hundred slaves," whose indulgence of them assures their affection and fidelity to his family (71–72, 189–90). The family's slave coachman, however, encouraged by northern men "of the lower order of democracy," asserts his right to freedom; but he is soon cowed "into shame and penitence, . . . I never do so again, Miss Lora, long I live," he says tearfully; "I wouldn't leave you for all the fine things in Yankee country. Bad folks put bad things in nigger's head" (247–53).

The narrator of Hentz's novel is a southerner, who at one point converses with a northerner about slavery as the South's hereditary destiny, and into this conversation he brings the remarkable story of George Horton. Mrs. Hentz appends a footnote to this conversation in which she insists on the authenticity of George and of her role in correcting and transcribing his poems. The southern narrator recalls how Horton learned to read and compose poetry, he recites excerpts from three of Horton's poems, and he describes the slave poet as "another Burns." "The lips of George," he says, "have been bathed with pure Castalian dew. He is a legitimate child of the muses." The northerner, upon hearing the narrator read one of Horton's verses, responds: "Astonishing! . . . there is an elevation of thought, and a delicacy of expression equally remarkable, when contrasted with the dull degraded intellect of his tribe." Thus, for both the southerner and northerner in the fiction, George Horton is a curiosity, a freakish talented exception, as he was for Chapel Hill students. *Lovell's Folly* is a novel; therefore, George's career ends happily and enforces the writer's moral: George has "panted for liberty, . . . and his prayers have been granted," the heroine says; her kind grandfather so admired George's poetry that he granted his slave freedom when he came "of age" if he promised to go to Liberia. George came of age but stayed on the plantation because "his affections are even stronger than his hopes. He is faithful, grateful, and unpretending, and looks as superior to his tribe, as your imagination can picture him. Instead of the broad smile of the African, he has the mild gravity of a Grecian philosopher" (253–60).

However misguided, patronizing, and racist her views, Caroline Hentz did try to help Horton. In 1828, she sent a letter with two of his poems, "Liberty and Slavery" and "On Poetry and Music" to her hometown newspaper, the Lancaster *Gazette*, and the paper published them on April 8 and on June 24, respectively. It is likely that she also participated in Horton's bid for freedom in 1828, and perhaps it was she who transcribed the twenty-one verses for Horton's first book, *The Hope of Liberty*. Without doubt, Horton was grateful to Hentz. In 1827, when her three-year-old son died from a fall that broke his neck, the poet dictated a "dirge" that brought her to tears and brought the poet "much credit and a handsome reward," he wrote. When she left the university in 1831, Horton regretted "the loss of her aid, which I shall never forget in life. At her departure from Chapel Hill, she left behind her the laurel of Thalia blooming on my mind, and went with all the spotless gaiety of Euphrosyne with regard to the signal services which she had done me." In gratitude, he wrote a poem called "Eulogy" for this "immortal dame": In the poem, Horton says she will surely outlast both the natural world and "the poet's task," until "Time's final shock" elevates her "to eternal fame." Almost thirty years later, in his "Address" Horton praised Hentz "for the signal favors conferred on me."

Horton's poetic fame spread from Hentz's Lancaster *Gazette*, back to North Carolina, and north again to New York and Massachusetts. In 1828, a "philanthropic gentleman," a member of an annual visitation board, came to Chapel Hill. Impressed with Horton's verse, he sent a brief sketch of Horton with "On the Evening and Morning" to the Raleigh *Register*, which published them on July 18, 1828. On the same date, "Slavery. By a Carolinian Slave named George Horton" appeared in the New York *Freedom's Journal*, the first newspaper in the nation to be published by African Americans. The newspaper, founded in 1827 by the Reverend Samuel Cornish and John Russwurm, declared its goals in the March 16, 1827 issue: "to further the cause of Black people through education, economic development, improved civil rights, literary development, greater knowledge of Africa and destruction of slavery." *Freedom's Journal* embraced the goal of Horton's freedom on August 8, 1828, with a brief front-page notice of a slave with "poetic talent," followed on August 29 with Horton's poem "On the Poetic Muse." Accompanying the poem were an editorial note informing readers that "measures are about to be taken to effect the emancipation" of the poet, plus an extract from their North Carolina correspondent's report. The extract states that George's owner has declined to sell his slave now—he is needed for "manual labor"—but might do so "towards the close of the year"; therefore, the reporter conveys the request of his friend, a "philanthropic gentleman," for "help of our northern friends" to obtain "from some of your benevolent societies, or by voluntary contribution, assistance in paying the price his master may demand for him." This price, "a sum like 4 or $500," the reporter wrote, cannot be raised in North Carolina—"It is contrary to the policy of the country"; thus, "the sympathies of New-York" are essential. The previous week's *Freedom's Journal* had provided an ironic comment on the correspondent's report, an announcement of the September meeting of the Manumission Society of North Carolina. On October 7, 1828, the Raleigh *Register* reported the Manumission Society's interest in Horton and printed his poem "On Hearing of the Intention of a Gentleman to Purchase the Poet's Freedom," but the Manumission Society took no action on behalf of the slave poet.

In the meantime, the September 5 issue of *Freedom's Journal* published Horton's "Gratitude," a poem he dedicated "to the Gentlemen [*sic*] who takes so kind an interest in his behalf." Horton's poetic vision here of the "dawn of Liberty" was premature, for the campaign by *Freedom's Journal* was not going well. A September 12 editorial reminded readers of the slave's dire need: "*Something must be done—George M. Horton must be liberated from a state of bondage.*" If each New Yorker "of colour" would "give but one penny," or, failing that, if those "disposed to give a little" would send in their names, we could aid this young man whose talents will be buried "if he is doomed to waste the prime of his days in vile servitude. Cannot one or two hundred dollars be raised towards purchasing his freedom?" Dollars did not flow in, but *Freedom's Journal* persisted: an editorial on October 3 announced "David C. Walker of Boston, Mass. as a subscriber to the fund" for Horton's manumission. David Walker, the Boston agent for *Freedom's Journal* during its two-year existence, was born in 1785 in North Carolina to a slave father and free mother and was therefore free to travel in the South, witnessing and hating the horrors of slavery. By 1825 he settled in Boston, where his eloquent lectures and writings against slavery culminated in publication of his incendiary pamphlet, *David Walker's Appeal in Four Articles* (1829). In June 1830, Walker was found dead, presumably poisoned. An editorial in *Freedom's Journal* of October 3, 1828, vainly appealed to Walker's "example" and readers' Christian values as well as their racial and northern pride to buy Horton's liberty. And on this note, the paper ended its campaign for the poet's freedom fund.

Southern efforts to gain Horton his freedom during the same summer months of 1828 had no better outcome. The Raleigh *Register*, on August 1, 5, and 8, printed three of Horton's poems. Influential friends took an interest: Joseph Gales, editor of the *Register*, and three men whom Horton praised in his "Address," namely, "Dr. [Joseph] Caldwell," for his "honor and humanity"; "Dr. James Henderson of Waynesboro"; and "the honorable and much distinguished" governor of North Carolina, John Owen.[17] Governor Owen, Horton recalled,

> descended like a dove to my assistance and exerted himself for my extrication from the distracting yoke of bondage. He cast a smile of unusual compassion on my condition which I never shall forget while I have the power of memory. He made an extraordinary proposition which was refused with a frown of disdain. . . . to pay [James Horton] $100 more than any person of sound judgment should say that I was worth. To this my master would not accede. Such was the miscarriage of the proposition from the feeling governor to a man who had no regard for liberty, science, or genius, not even a spark of generosity then pervaded his iron heart (8).

Nevertheless, Horton and his supporters determined to raise funds sufficient to secure his freedom by selling a twenty-two page volume of twenty-one poems entitled *The Hope of Liberty*. The publisher was Joseph Gales, a transplanted North Carolinian, secretary of the regional American Colonization Society. Gales's "Explanation," introducing the volume, assures readers that George's emancipation is conditioned upon "his going in the vessel which shall first afterwards sail for Liberia. It is his earnest and only wish to become a member of that Colony." However, no evidence exists that Horton ever wished to colonize Liberia; indeed, he declared in "My Native Home" (1865), "fair Columbia, thou art mine." Both slaveholders and many abolitionists supported colonization, but by 1865 the Colonization Society had settled only 5,500 emancipated slaves in Liberia, primarily because African Americans did not want to emigrate. Gales promised to send Horton to Liberia because colonization was a popular way to rid the state of freed slaves, and Gales was selling books (and his own pro-colonization views). To further attract buyers, Gales's "Explanation" presents "George" as a legally-owned and worthy cause: "the property of Mr. James Horton"; a home-grown amateur poet, whose blemished but original poems were "all written down by others"; and a law-abiding rustic who read and composed poems only at night and at other "usual intervals allowed to slaves," for he "has ever been a faithful, honest and industrious slave." The publisher designated his son, Weston R. Gales, to collect the proceeds from sales of *The Hope of Liberty*, which appeared in July 1829; but this historic volume, the first book published by an African American in the South, earned scarcely any profit, at least not for its author.

Although Horton did not earn enough from *Hope of Liberty* to buy his freedom, the very publication of this volume attests to the liberal atmosphere in North Carolina, and especially in Chapel Hill. Nowhere else in the South would the antislavery views of Judge William Gaston have been as welcomed as they were at the University of North Carolina in 1832. Gaston, a former congressman and current trustee of the university, delivered a commencement address to the Dialectic and Philosophic societies in which he praised the U.S. Constitution, denounced disunion, and advocated the abolition of slavery, which "stifles industry and represses enterprise— . . . it impairs our strength as a community, and poisons morals at the fountain head." Not only did the Chapel Hill audience heartily cheer Gaston, but his published speech was reprinted five times before 1849. And six months after his 1832 speech, the General Assembly elected Gaston a Supreme Court judge.[18]

Poet Horton benefited from the relative open-mindedness at the university, the support of president Joseph Caldwell, for whom he worked, and his popularity with the students. He was earning three to four dollars a week from sales of his love poems, an extraordinary sum at a time when a student's monthly allowance was $1.00 and his weekly board $2.50; fresh meat sold for 4 or 5 cents a pound and eggs for 8 to 10 cents a dozen; and an acre of university land cost $100.[19] Horton's lucrative trade in verse as well as his dislike of farm labor led him to hire his time from James Horton in about 1833. Although it was prohibited by law, his master sold Horton his time for twenty-five cents a week, leaving the poet with a substantial profit.

During the 1830s, Horton unknowingly contributed to the abolition movement when his verse circulated in the North. In 1837, *The Hope of Liberty* traveled from Cincinnati into the hands of two Philadelphia abolitionists, Joshua Coffin and then Lewis Gunn. Gunn changed the title to *Poems by a Slave* and published the volume in Philadelphia, including Joseph Gales's 1829 introduction and a new "Preface" by Gunn. This preface reminded readers that although Gales was "*no abolitionist*," he had admitted the evils of slavery, the slaves' unhappiness, and George's sensitivity to his bondage. Gunn also included a letter from Joshua Coffin confirming that George was still "the slave of James

Horton" and "has attended to other occupations" since "his patron" President Caldwell died. The last statement confirms what is known, that for almost two decades Horton had supplemented his income from poetry by doing odd jobs for Joseph Caldwell and that after Caldwell's death in 1835, Horton worked for students and faculty of Chapel Hill as a handyman and servant. Another edition of *The Hope of Liberty* was published in Boston in 1838 by Isaac Knapp, publisher of William Lloyd Garrison's *Liberator*. Knapp's "third" edition was appended to *Memoir and Poems of Phillis Wheatley* with an introduction that pleaded for the education and religious instruction of slaves in order to prepare them for emancipation. Knapp's 1838 edition offered a lengthy biography of Wheatley but only the prefatory materials from the two earlier editions of *The Hope of Liberty*.

Horton's poems also appeared occasionally in northern and southern periodicals. In one instance, the *Southern Literary Messenger* of April 1843 printed his "Lines to My ——" and "Ode to Liberty," sent in from Chapel Hill. The sender, "G.," perhaps Professor Ralph Henry Graves Sr. or Professor William Mercer Green, said the poems came from "a volume of manuscript Poems [that was] lately placed in my hands by their author, George Horton, a negro boy."[20] This volume may have been Horton's *The Poetical Works* (1845), but the anonymous introduction to that book refers to another manuscript volume called *The Museum*. Furthermore, an anonymous writer in 1860 said he had seen the "manuscript of another book of his [Horton's] poems [that] contains 229 pages letter-paper closely written," with a lengthy subscription list.[21] And in 1929, Collier Cobb recalled that "in the late 80's" he had received from his great-uncle "a manuscript of Horton's, prepared while he was still at the University"; Cobb said he gave this manuscript to the university library "a few years ago," but it could not be found when he went to retrieve it.[22] None of these manuscript volumes of poems has ever been located and probably none was printed.

The "negro boy" whom "G" introduced to the *Messenger* in 1843 was then about forty-six years old. Sometime in the previous decade, Horton had married a slave of Franklin Snipes, a Chatham farmer, and had sired two children, a son, Free Snipes, who lived in Raleigh in 1888 and died in Durham in 1896, and a daughter, Rhody, who married Van Buren Byrum, lived in Chapel Hill until about 1878, and resided in Raleigh in 1897.[23] Nothing more is known about Horton's wedded life or his descendants. Indeed, since Horton's autobiography in *The Poetical*

Works stops abruptly at the year 1831, almost no facts illumine the next half century of his life. However, several significant events in Horton's life between 1840 and 1860 are documented. In the summer of 1843, his master, James, died and left his property to four sons. George's new master was Hall Horton, a thirty-three-year-old bachelor, a tanner by trade, who farmed a few hundred acres "on the stage road in the Trades Hill section of Chatham."[24] Hall Horton raised his slave's hire fee to fifty cents. The higher fee; the need to acclimate himself once again to a new master; and the bondage of almost half a century that seemed ever more inimical to the poet's art may have motivated George Horton to try again for liberty, first with the proceeds from another published volume and then with pleading letters.

If Horton's bids for freedom in the relatively liberal climate of the 1820s had failed, his renewed efforts surely were doomed in the atmosphere of fear and repression that dominated the decades after 1830. Abolitionist activities in the North grew stronger and exacerbated sectional conflicts. From pulpits and podiums, in petitions and calls, at meetings of African American and interracial antislavery societies, and from black and white periodicals rose the clamor for abolition of slavery. Polemics and militant protest poetry fueled the flames, as did thousands of widely circulated slave narratives, vivid chronicles of slave life and dramatic escapes, written in the 1830s to 1850s by fugitives or from their dictation. As many former slaves, like Frederick Douglass, became celebrities of the lecture circuit and the press at home and abroad, their tales added to southerners' antagonism, terrors, and defensiveness.

North Carolina rallied to protect slavery against northern abolitionists, against the threat posed by the British Parliament's passage of a gradual emancipation act in 1832, and, above all, against slave insurrections throughout the region. In 1830, slaves fought patrols in eastern North Carolina with arson, and armed maroons plotted slave uprisings in half a dozen counties. As copies of David Walker's militant *Appeal* spread throughout the state, a slave uprising shocked Wilmington, Walker's native town, and was followed by months of severe unrest and violence there. Dread of an abolitionist conspiracy accompanied copies of Walker's pamphlet west to Fayetteville, east to New Bern, and north to Hillsborough counties. Governor Zebulon B. Owen sent copies of the *Appeal* to legislators, convincing them to offer a reward for Walker's capture, dead or alive. Another crisis came in August 1831, when Nat Turner led an insurrection of seventy slaves in Southampton, Virginia, on the northeast border of North Carolina. In forty-eight hours, the rebels killed sixty whites, unleashing an epidemic of panic and wholesale slaughter of slaves. In North Carolina, where non-slaveholding poor whites were suspected of aiding the Turner rebels, extravagant rumors of conspiracies and massacres by slaves frightened easterners for two months, and they jailed and whipped dozens of slaves and executed about twenty. Three North Carolina slaveholders died of fright, from heart failure, and North Carolinians pressed the governor to mobilize men and arms and wrote to him that they lashed and hung their restless slaves; martial law was declared in Raleigh in November. The repercussions of Turner's rebellion in North Carolina were extreme: "the panic, exaggerated reports, arrests, beatings, executions, and lynchings lasted well into November, 1831."[25] Nat Turner was hanged on November 11. News of these slave uprisings surely reached George Horton in Chapel Hill, but ever mindful of his status, a slave selling his poetry in the South, he never referred to slave unrest in his verse or prose.

In 1830–33 the North Carolina legislature enacted the strongest restrictions on slaves and free blacks in the state's history, with more stringent statutes to come in the following decades. Laws set heavy penalties for publishing or distributing antislavery materials. The first indictment under this law came in 1831, when a grand jury of the North Carolina Supreme Court indicted Garrison and Isaac Knapp (who later published Horton's *The Poetical Works*) for circulating an issue of the *Liberator* "containing the most reckless and unjustifiable allusions to the attempted insurrection amongst the Slaves in this state."[26] Unlike Horton's *The Hope of Liberty* (1829), *The Poetical Works* (1845) contained no antislavery poems, in keeping with the new repressive atmosphere and publishing restrictions. Other North Carolina statutes of 1830–33 enlarged the powers of slave patrols; prohibited slaves from raising domestic animals, selling spirits, gambling, preaching, hunting with a gun, buying and selling goods with other slaves or white men, and hiring their own time; and forbade the teaching of slaves to read or write. George Horton, a nonconformist among his peers, both hired his time and learned to read and write in violation of these laws. Statutes of this period also restricted the free black population of North Carolina, which was larger than in any other southern state except Virginia and Maryland. In 1835, the North Carolina Constitutional Convention disenfranchised free blacks as well as free persons "of mixed blood, descended from negro ancestors, to the fourth generation inclusive," thus revoking the rights guaranteed to free men by the U.S. Constitution.[27] North Carolina's legal suppression of its African American populations in the 1830s was followed by national arguments in 1846–60 over the extension of slavery: the Wilmot Proviso (1846), the Compromise debates (1850), the Kansas-Nebraska Act (1854) all generated controversies that divided North Carolinians into warring political camps. George Horton seemed well aware of current events, although he never versified them until the Civil War poems of *Naked Genius*. In his "Address" of 1859, however, he dared to comment on the political and economic turmoil in the nation: The nation's "productions have long been dwindling at the shrine of depreciation and exhausted commerce. . . . peace [has] sunk into the confusion of parties . . . [contending] for the rights of liberty and laws." He feared for "the dissolution of national union" and bewailed "a policy which set the Union in the fire of faction which still appears cannot be extinguished but with blood which must proceed from the hand of sectional havoc" (14). It is remarkable that this slave, speaking in public in the South, should expose his awareness of national ills and presciently warn of the coming Civil War.

As national legislation provoked ever-stronger secessionist sentiments among North Carolinians, changes in the state's slave population, economic conditions, and new slave revolts further strengthened proslavery forces. From 1840 to 1860 the number of slaves, free blacks, and large slaveholding plantations had increased significantly, giving North Carolina a greater stake in the slavery controversy, as did economic factors. The state's cotton culture grew more profitable; the average price of an acre of land rose from $2.27 in 1833 to $6.03 in 1860; and prices of prime field hands soared from an average of $425 in 1830 to $800 in 1840 to $1,600 in 1860.[28] The majority view of the value of slavery was expressed before the State Agricultural Society in 1855 by Thomas Ruffin, who was associate justice and chief justice of North Carolina's Supreme Court from 1829 to 1853 and a congressman from 1853 to 1861. Ruffin said: "Slavery here is favorable to the interests of agriculture in point of economy and profit, and not unwholesome to the moral and social condition of each race." Blacks, he said, are physically suited to labor in the North Carolina climate, and if freed they would soon sink into drunken, debauched savagery.[29]

Incidents of "savagery" again terrorized the populace in 1856 when armed slave uprisings spread throughout the South; the maroons, in particular, were dangerously active in North Carolina. In 1859, when John Brown and twelve whites and five blacks attacked the armory in Harpers Ferry, Virginia, North Carolina responded by organizing new military companies and strengthening its arms supplies. North Carolina's liberal attitudes toward slavery had shifted 180 degrees since 1829, as Robert Connor noted: "Between 1850 and 1860, the press, the bench, the church, the school, all surrendered to the demands of the slave power."[30] The Quakers, liberal politicians and newspapers, and emancipation societies now lost power, were shut down, or left the state. No antislavery sentiments, spoken or written, were allowed expression in North Carolina.

Two events of the 1850s illustrate the slavocracy's power. Benjamin Sherwood Hedrick was an 1851 honors graduate of the University of North Carolina, and in 1854 he became professor and chair of its agricultural chemistry department. In 1856, responding to a question, Hedrick said he would support the presidential ticket of John C. Fremont (the antislavery candidate) if one were offered in North Carolina. A student demanded the dismissal of this "Black Republican" professor, and Hedrick, in quiet, reasonable prose, explained his antislavery position. University students hung him in effigy; faculty disowned him; parents threatened to withdraw their sons; and alumni, the press, and the public called for the traitor's expulsion. University trustees dismissed Hedrick from his professorship, and, hounded by a mob, he shortly afterward left his native state.[31] The second event involved Hinton Rowan Helper (1829–1909), who, like Hedrick, was born in Rowan County of western North Carolina. In his book *The Impending Crisis of the South: How to Meet It* (1857), Helper (although neither a supporter or admirer of blacks) presented antislavery arguments from the point of view of a small farmer. He statistically compared the economic and social progress of North and South to show that slavery hindered the progress of southern states, and he asserted that wealthy slaveholders used slavery to sustain their dominance over lower-class whites. The blasphemous book was banned and burned in bonfires in North Carolina, and men who owned or circulated a copy, including four ministers, were denounced and jailed.

Like the state of North Carolina, the university shifted from liberalism to intolerance, from welcoming Gaston to dismissing Hedrick in a few decades. From the mid-1830s to 1860, it underwent many changes, including the death of president Joseph Caldwell in 1835 and his replacement by David L. Swain, who led the renewal of the university. Swain, who was from a prominent North Carolina family on his mother's side, studied and practiced law in the state and served in the House of Commons In 1832, the General Assembly elected him governor of North Carolina, the youngest man ever to hold that office. Reelected to one-year terms in 1833 and 1834, Swain was by all accounts an able, practical, diplomatic, and bold governor. During his long tenure in Chapel Hill, president Swain raised admission and academic standards, stabilized failing finances, upgraded faculty and physical plant, established many curricula and disciplinary reforms, and increased esteem for UNC in the state and nation. Personally, Swain was a popular president, a man of integrity, "genial temper, ready wit, . . . [and] kindliness." He was known as "lenient" to his children and slaves, but as his dealings with Horton revealed, Swain was in all things prudential, ever cautious and discreet, seemingly fearful of offending anyone.[32]

George Horton might have been a free man two decades before emancipation if Caldwell rather than Swain had been president of the university in the 1840s. On September 3, 1844, Horton wrote a letter to William Lloyd Garrison, the radical abolitionist most despised and reviled throughout the South. Horton appealed to Garrison's love of genius and curiosity "in resolving the problem whether a Negro has any genius or not." Garrison knew of Horton; ten years earlier the *Liberator* (March 29) had printed "On Liberty and Slavery" with Garrison's introductory note, linking Horton to the growing "talents of the degraded race of black people" such as the Haitian revolutionaries and the "few individuals [who] have sprung up amid darkness and misfortunes." A "good education," Garrison concluded, would surely raise the race high among nations. However unlikely it was that the slave had read the abolitionist's note, Horton's letter of 1844 plays up to Garrison's views, with assurances that his motives for writing poetry were not solely "pecuniary . . . but, upon the whole, to spread the blaze of African genius and thus dispel the sceptic gloom, so prevalent in many parts of the country." With characteristic immodesty, Horton related how his genius developed through "resolution" despite lack of a formal education; he deprecated his reading and writing skills and "clouded" intellect; and he trusted that the "facts of my condition" would inspire

Garrison "to open to the world a volume which like a wild bird has long been struggling in its shell, impatient to transpire to the eye of a dubious world." Horton entrusted the mailing of this letter to President David Swain, who filed the poet's appeal to Garrison among his papers, where it remains today.

Undaunted by the absence of a reply from Garrison, in the summer of 1845 Horton and his supporters circulated a subscription list in Chapel Hill for publication of a new volume of verse. The list of ninety-nine subscribers, printed in *The Poetical Works*, included eighty-one UNC students, the mayor of Chapel Hill, President Swain, and other local notables. In the autumn, Dennis Heartt, a former New Englander who was editor of the Hillsborough *Recorder*, published *The Poetical Works of George M. Horton, the Colored Bard of North-Carolina.* The introduction insisted that the poet was "deeply conscious of his own inferiority" to other ancient and modern poets and was motivated to write only "by pleasure and curiousity [*sic*], . . . or as an example to remove the doubts of cavilists with regard to African genius." Because of the poet's rude upbringing and educational deprivations, the anonymous writer continued, Horton's genius "is but an unpolished diamond, and can never shine forth to the world." Attuned to the proslavery temper of the times, the introduction and almost all the poems in *The Poetical Works* sidestepped the subjects of slavery and Horton's hopes for freedom. *The Poetical Works* was bargain-priced at fifty cents, the cost of only one or two of the poet's love verses; but as before, sales did not yield sufficient funds to buy Horton from bondage.

Northern abolitionists had not forgotten "The Slave Poet": a brief tribute to him with that title appeared in the *National Anti-Slavery Standard* in 1846. The writer lamented: "What must his tender poetic heart have endured through these long weary years of bondage. Who can bear to think of his sufferings?" After a fervid plea for "liberation of the American slaves" came Horton's 1829 poem "'The Slave's Complaint' By an American Slave." In the fifteen years after *The Poetical Works* was published, Horton hired his time and somehow survived as poet, servant, and odd-jobs man at the university, alternating, perhaps, with work on his master's farm. "The slave poet," Kemp Battle wrote, "flourished from 1840 to 1860. . . . Horton was of medium height, dark, but not black. His manner was courteous, his moral character good. Like Byron, Burns and Poe he often quenched the divine spark with unpoetic whiskey."[33] Thomas Miles Garrett was in his second year at UNC when he wrote in his diary for July 4, 1849: We had a celebration here on the "Hill"; the students "thought that they would not let the 'forth' [*sic*] pass without some noise, and accordingly held a meeting and appointed George Haughton [*sic*] alias the N. Carolina bard to deliver the oration. This morning the poet arrived and about 11 O'clock we formed a procession and conducted the orator upon the stage. He made a speech of about 5 minutes length, to the great disappointment of all present, who expected a long oration. The loud, long, and repeated applause occupied however about fifteen minutes."[34] Once again, the slave, now over fifty years old, was put on display.

A more admirable display of Horton's keen mind and grasp of current events also occurred in 1849. The December 29 issue of the Raleigh *Register* contained his spirited defense of American literature, of "native talent" over "foreign" products, a defense that echoed the cultural nationalism of America's most prominent writers from Philip Freneau through Ralph Waldo Emerson and beyond. The *Register* had welcomed Louis Kossuth, the president-elect of Hungary, and included some British poetry in his honor; Horton responded: "I am for developing *our own* resources, and cherishing native genius. . . . As a North Carolina patriot, I ask, Why leave our own to stand on foreign soil? Why *go abroad* for poetry when we have an infinitely superior article of domestic manufacture? I am too modest to speak of my own, but surely there *is* poetry of native growth, even of your fair City of Oaks, good enough for a Toast to Louis Kossuth, without straying off into foreign parts."[35] These were not the words of an ignorant slave but of a poet, proud of the calling he shared with contemporary American writers.

In 1852, George Horton was fifty-five years old; yet over half a century of bondage had not dimmed his hopes for liberty. At this time Hall Horton may have at last agreed to sell his aged slave because the poet wrote to David Swain, begging the president to buy him in order, it seems, to alleviate his arduous eight-mile commute from the farm to the campus; for Horton wrote: "Sir, my object for this is my distant walk to attend to my business, which chiefly lies on the Hill. The price is $250, which I cannot but think I am worth." Horton promised to serve Swain "to the best of my ability" and "to make you all the possible remuneration which I can," provided that his "books" of poetry were published. "Please write a note to Master," the letter ended, with the signature, "George M. Horton / Poet." Swain filed the letter, as before, and told Horton to write to Horace Greeley, editor of the New York *Tribune*; that is, in his letter to Greeley, Horton *said* that Swain told him to write. On September 11, 1852, the poet applied to Greeley's "beneficent hand for some assistance to remove the burden of hard servitude." He asked for $175—had Hall Horton dropped his price?—and again promised to repay the sum when his publications paid off. Horton detailed his credentials: "I am the only public or recognized poet of color in my native state or perhaps in the union, born in slavery but yet craving that scope and expression whereby my literary labor of the night may be circulated throughout the whole world." The plea ended with Horton's favorite poetic image of the genius "confined in these loathsome fetters" set free to "soar as an eagle" if only Greeley would assist the "lowering vassal" to arise. On the back of this letter, Horton wrote a poem entitled "The Poet's Feeble Petition," repeating his plea. In this piece, Horton employed complex contradictory images of a ruthless, deaf, stony-hearted world that fetters a feeble, penitential slave; the speaker asks for pity, but at the same time he asserts his pride and self-esteem—in spite of all, he is a Bard, an aspiring eagle, a singer in the valley, a genius, and gifted Negro. Once more Horton entrusted the letter for mailing to David Swain, who buried it in his papers.

The slave's final effort—at least it is the last Horton letter found in Swain's files—is a follow-up to his earlier request that Swain buy him for $250. Sent to Swain through a student named John T. Gilmore, the undated note reiterated Horton's proposition, and now promised Swain "two-thirds on the whole of the proceeds of my book now preparing for the press." He assured Swain that subscriptions for the book were coming in, and the president "never will sustain any loss" by granting this request. Swain did not respond, and the "fettered genius" waited another dozen years for emancipation.

Among George Horton's last recorded accomplishments before the war were two published poems: "What is Time," which appeared in the Chapel Hill *Gazette* on May 9, 1857, and an old favorite, "On Liberty and Slavery," published in the *Emancipator* on October 12, 1857. His most unusual achievement was the twenty-nine-page oration "An Address. The Stream of Liberty and Science . . .," which Horton delivered in UNC's Gerrard Hall in 1859 to "young gentlemen of the Freshman class." Since many different students copied down parts of Horton's address while he spoke it, the manuscript is difficult to read, words are

Septr 11 1852 Chapel Hill
To Mr Greely N C

sir
from the information of the president of the
of the university of north carolina to wit
the honorable D. L. swain who is willing to
aid me himself I learn that you are a gentleman
of philanthropic feeling I therefore thought
thought it essential to apply to your beneficent
hand for some assistance to remove the burden
of hard servitude notwithstanding sir there
are many in my native state and county who wish
to bring me out and there are others far too penurious
which renders it somewhat dubious with regard
to my extrication it is evident that you have
heard of me by the fame of my works in poetry much
of which I am now too closely confined to carry out and
which I feel a warm interest to do and sir by
favouring me with the bounty of 175 dollars
I will endeavour to reward your generosity with
my productions as soon as possible I am the
only publick or recognized poet of colour in
my native state or perhaps in the union
born in slavery but yet craving that scope and
expression whereby my literary labour of the
night may be circulated throughout the whole
world then o forbid that my productions
should ever fall to the ground but rather
soar as an eagle above the towering mountains
and thus return as a triumphing spirit to the
bosom of its God who gave it birth though
now confined in these loathsome fetters
please assist the towering vassal to arise and
live a glad denizen the remnant of his days
and one of active utility yours respect

George M Horton
of colour

Letter to Horace Greeley, September 11, 1852, David Lowry Swain Papers, Southern Historical Collection, University of North Carolina, Chapel Hill missing, and its overall accuracy is questionable. Nevertheless, on one hand, the "Address" is a rambling, repetitive accumulation of disconnected comments on Horton's privations and need for liberty; his visions of judgment day and a reborn world; fatherly advice to students; praise of learning and knowledge; political opinions; and snatches of poetry. The language and tone range from high poetic and prophetic to colloquial, all spiced with pretentious rhetorical flourishes, proverbs, learned allusions, and biblical quotations. Aware of his oratorical defects, Horton asks the audience to pity his "tautological constipation or seraphic flights from the topic."

On the other hand, the "Address" offers some important insights into Horton's heart and mind in his sixty-second year. He begins: "Actuated by innocent motives, I appear before you, as a public orator in the cause of Liberty and Science, but with a degree of diffidence lest I fail to accomplish a task which I feel it my duty to discharge." His central purpose is to champion "Liberty with her exalted train of sciences, which converts fools into sages, the heathen into Christians, and men into angels" (21). By "sciences" he means all areas of knowledge: Horton praises progress gained through navigation, railroading, and agriculture, and he compliments students' grasp of history, geography, astronomy, and geology. But, he insists, the most valuable science is theology; it is essentially tied to liberty, for theology graduates must "bear the orthodox tenets of Christianity" to the heathen, to raise them from "wickedness and vice, . . . savage anarchy and their ignorance of liberal education" (10, 16, 19). Horton expressed the same view of theology in his poem of 1831, "The Pleasures of College Life." Assuming the role of proxy-parent or minister, Horton exhorts youths who "have gone astray like Ephriam to his idols or the rebellious Israelites" to avoid vanities, pleasures, "the shrine of tottering Bacchus"—all follies that detract from pursuit of knowledge and "culture of faculties rational" which ensure liberty and national greatness (4–5, 7). Interspersed with such high-minded advice are Horton's musings on his own deprivations; for example, Why was he "in a shell of bastardy deposited by an itinerant muse at the foot of a mountain . . . deserted at the close of her incubation and left . . . without the plumage of literary defence, waiting in vain for her return with a morsel to sustain the infancy of genius. . . . Did Clio scorn the hue of his products, or did Erato pluck a string from her lyre and leave it floating on the stream of chance like the Hebrew foundling [Moses] in the rush ark, or why is he thus un-

662591

The Stream of Liberty and Science

Gentlemen

Actuated by innocent motives. I appear
before you, as a public Orator in the cause of Liberty
and Science; but with a degree of diffidence lest I
fail to accomplish a task which I feel it my duty
to discharge. Your unworthy speaker is far from flatt-
ering himself, with the vain idea of being endowed
talent abilities to counsel a concourse on so lofty a
where superior liberties afford them so many
tunate advantages. Yet while you laugh to
his ignorance, he still is constrained from
a impulse of illiterate genius to expose his jargon
to the criticism of the world, it is obvious that we
occupy an age of the world which calls aloud for
literary improvement from every quarter and the
scientific culture of faculties rational. nay as well
from the rustic swain in the lonely valley, as the
Epicure on luxuriant streams. is it not aspired to
in the present age, for impartial genius seems to
have looked with an indiscriminate eye as touching
nations and color and directed her headlong torrents
which have swept in their course the wandering
novice, who could scarcely distinguish a letter from a
figure. We see many possessed with superior advantages
which they cast off as nonsense, whilst others far
less promoted are gleaning up the scattered fragments
with avidity and have thus augmented a wonderful
store of intellectual matter, compiled and original and
contributed to the scenes of public admiration, to
ascend the glorious summit of mental improvement
is first to arouse your minds from every degree
of lethargy to an active application of close study and

Pages one and eight of "An Address. The Stream of Liberty and Science. To Collegiates of the University of N.C. By George M. Horton The Black Bard," 1859, North Carolina Collection, University of North Carolina, Chapel Hill

8

on me from the liberal hand of the celebrated
Mrs Caroline Lee Hentz. But my theme of gratitude
stops not here. The honorable and much distinguished
Gov. Owen now deceased developed a stream of surpassing
humanity. far from the information of
the much esteemed Dr James Henderson of
Waynesboro. he descended like a dove to my
assistance and exerted himself for my
extrication from the distracting yoke of
bondage. He cast a smile of unusual com-
passion on my condition which I never shall
forget. While I have the power of memory.
He made an extraordinary proposition which
was refused with a frown of disdain. The
proposition was to pay $100, more than any
person of sound judgment should say that I
was worth, So thus my master would not
accede, Such was the miscarriage of
the proposition from the feeling Governor
to a man who had no regard for
liberty science or Genius, not even a spark
of generosity then pervaded his countenance
A smile of generosity from a few individ-
uals seldom prevails, amidst the unanimous
frowns of thousands who point at
the slightest faults in genius as an
enormous crime, Gentlemen I trust
that your patience will hold out a little
farther and pardon the irresistable
circumstances which had unexpectedly
fallen in my way so let me terminate this
part of my topic with an uncommon
preceding the next, A good name is better
than precious ointment and the day of
death than the day of ones birth

fortunate." Horton does not answer his questions except to say that he will not blame others because "every tub has to stand on its own bottom and not on that of another" (6–7).

In "The Pleasures of College Life" Horton expresses how he felt at home in the university and embraces with great respect and enjoyment its intellectual bounty; but three decades later he seems estranged and embittered. The "Address" reveals his deep anguish at being an "illiterate genius" speaking to students with "superior liberties" and "superior advantages" for learning that they carelessly cast off, while he merely gleans "up the scattered fragments with avidity." Horton laments that his lot was cast in a rude life of illiteracy and labor "rather than in a repository of Belle Letters with others who thirst for liberal instruction" (1, 5, 6). As in his poems, he equates physical with intellectual liberty, and his voice is filled with regret, envy, and a resigned sadness after almost forty years of servitude at the university. If this "Address" were attributed to a university student or professor, it would rightly be criticized as pretentious, disorganized, rhetorically overblown, and even, in its visionary fancies, somewhat mad. What then can be said of these extemporaneous flights of moral, academic, and personal wisdom coming from the lowly slave? Oddly enough, taken in small doses, Horton's "Address" communicates power and sincerity; today's reader can only marvel at passages of sound reasoning and practical advice; at imaginative mergings of present and future events; at the breadth of learning from books and knowledge of current events; and at the sheer nerve and verve of poet Horton.

It seems that Horton's life at the university did not change in the decades leading up to the Civil War, even though change took place all around him. By 1860, North Carolina was no longer the "Rip Van Winkle State": it had reformed its educational, social, and political institutions and made vast improvements in transportation, agriculture, industry, and banking, while constitutional amendments produced more democratic electoral policies. The "stream of liberty" ran faster for Horton and American slavery after Abraham Lincoln's election in 1860. North Carolina joined the Confederate States of America in May 1861 and contributed significantly to the Civil War effort. During the war, many thousands of slaves ran away from their masters to fight for the Union. Others "fought" on the Confederate side: hired or impressed, they labored in factories, mines, and mills, and on roads, fortifications, and railroads; or they accompanied their masters to war as servants and entertainers, or served as nurses, drivers, and laborers for the Confederacy. George Horton stayed home.

At his "alma mater," enrollments, which had increased steadily up to 1859, swiftly declined: in 1860–61, 155 out-of-state students left for the army when their states voted to secede, and North Carolina students, both volunteers and conscripts, soon followed. In 1862, only 100 students were enrolled, and by the fall term of 1864, 47 students remained.[36] The war ruined the university financially, so that by 1866, faculty salaries could not be paid; the university was $110,000 in debt, its buildings had deteriorated, and its entire endowment was lost through the insolvency of the Bank of North Carolina. With the university depleted of students and resources, Horton lost the market for his services and poems. In his late sixties now, he most likely sat out the war on Hall Horton's farm.

On April 17, 1865, General Smith B. Atkins led the 9th Michigan Cavalry Volunteers into Chapel Hill, which they occupied until May 3. There are two versions of George Horton's movements in the spring of 1865, both of them bringing Horton under the patronage of Captain William H. S. Banks of the 9th Michigan Cavalry Volunteers. Banks was responsible for the publication of Horton's final volume, *Naked Genius*, probably in the late summer of 1865. In his introduction to this volume, Banks wrote that he met Horton "during the victorious march of our army through the State of North Carolina, . . . [Horton was] one of the many refugees who flocked to our lines for safety." In his "Sketch of the Author," Banks further said that Horton "escaped to our lines for protection" when the Michigan Cavalry occupied Raleigh. That is, by Banks's account, early in April, several weeks before emancipation was announced in Chapel Hill, Horton walked the thirty miles to Raleigh, found Banks, and returned to Chapel Hill with the cavalry on April 17. Another version of these events recorded by Richard Walser claimed that Horton stayed in Chapel Hill until Banks arrived and met him there.

In any case, testimony of Banks and evidence from Horton's poems confirm that the twenty-eight-year-old captain and the sixty-eight-year-old poet traveled together as Banks's regiment moved west out of Chapel Hill in May to Greensboro and Lexington (see "Execution of Private Henry Anderson"; the private killed a civilian on May 9 in Greensboro and was executed in Lexington on May 11). In June they traveled to Concord (see "The Late Thunder Storm in Camp at Concord, N.C. June 20, 1865"). Banks and Horton then backtracked to Lexington, where on July 21 the 9th Cavalry was released from service; afterward they traveled east to Raleigh. In Raleigh, William B. Smith published *Naked Genius by George Moses Horton, The Colored Bard of North Carolina.* For Horton the three-month physical journey alone was an amazing feat: a man nearing seventy had walked almost 300 miles and had lived precariously in army camps in the heat of May, June, and July. Undoubtedly, his mental and emotional journeys were as arduous, for as he walked and camped, Horton composed *ninety* new poems for *Naked Genius.* Banks reported that he worked "both night and day composing poems for his book" and that he also wrote "acrostics for the boys on their sweethearts' names, in which he takes great delight." The "unfettered" slave surely enjoyed his freedom to versify, but many poems in *Naked Genius* suggest how difficult Horton found these months on the road among strangers. After a lifetime in bondage, for him a restrictive but protective environment, Horton missed the familiar small world of the Chatham farm and the eight miles of countryside to Chapel Hill. Many poems in *Naked Genius,* like "The Southern Refugee," express longing for home, family, and friends in the voice of the poet himself, or voices of soldiers displaced by war; the word "home" appears in the titles of seven poems.

Naked Genius was the last documented product of Horton's pen. Banks said that Horton showed him "manuscripts written by himself," and on the title page of *Naked Genius* he credited Horton as "Author of 'The Black Poet,' a work now being compiled and revised. . . which will be ready for publication about the 1st of October, 1865." "The Black Poet" will contain a life history of the author, wrote Banks, and will prove to the public "that God, in His infinite wisdom and mercy, created the black man for a higher and nobler purpose than to toil his life away under the galling yoke of slavery." At the end of *Naked Genius,* Banks again promoted "The Black Poet"; he appealed for "energetic young men," especially those disabled by the war, to "build up a fortune for themselves" by selling the soon-to-appear book. And once more Banks offered a spirited defense of black men who "are really possessed of genius, which when properly cultivated will elevate and prepare them to assume the grave responsibilities of" their emancipated condition. In these pages, Banks consistently and sincerely defends the potential of all freedmen, and he enthusiastically admires Horton's art; therefore, his desertion of "Mr. Horton" is all the more regrettable. Even before *Naked Genius* appeared, Banks returned to Lawton, Michigan, the address given in his appeal for salesman. And the promised new volume, "The Black Poet," was never published.

It is presumed that Horton traveled north from Raleigh to Philadelphia, Pennsylvania, sometime in 1866. Where and how Horton lived in the following eighteen years and where he died are unknown. Stephen Weeks quotes from the "published minutes of the Banneker Institute," given to him by Daniel Murray of the Library of Congress; his extract says: "A special meeting of the institution was held on the evening of August 31, 1866 [in Philadelphia], the object being to receive Mr. George Horton of North Carolina, a poet of considerable genius, it was claimed. The feasibility of publishing his book was submitted to Mr. John H. Smythe, but found too expensive."[37] Neither the minutes of this meeting nor the short stories Weeks claims Horton sold to Philadelphia periodicals can be found. Collier Cobb, a native North Carolinian and geology professor at Chapel Hill, wrote in 1929 that he had "called on Poet Horton in Philadelphia in 1883, the very year in which he died." Horton, Cobb reported, was then "publishing short stories in a number of newspapers" and occasionally had been employed by three members of the Cobb family in Philadelphia. And Cobb recalled, "I called him 'Poet,' which pleased him greatly, and he told me that I was using his proper title."[38] However, forty-three years earlier Cobb had delivered a paper about Horton in which he did *not* mention his visit to the poet in 1883. Rather, Cobb's paper of 1886 offered second-hand descriptions, hearsay, some incorrect details, and unsupported assertions about Horton. Cobb said that in Philadelphia Horton was writing modernized Bible stories and poetry remotely influenced by "Elizabethan poets" Marlowe and Raleigh; Horton "did very little work before reaching the age of forty, and the most productive period of his life began when he was sixty-seven years old, continuing to the close of his life, at the age of eighty-five, in 1883."[39] As Merle Richmond has rightly pointed out, Cobb offered no references to or examples of Horton's poems, stories, or other late works, although Cobb's "was ostensibly a scholarly paper."[40] It is unfortunate that Cobb's suppositions and his conclusion that "George never really cared for more liberty than he had, but he was fond of playing to the grand-stand" infected writings about Horton for the next half century. Regrettable, too, is Cobb's failure to disclose where, or exactly when, or how Horton died, although it seems that he knew these details. The Death Records of

Philadelphia (1878–84), which Walser consulted, do not record Horton's death. Overall, then, we know only that after 1866 poet Horton lived in Philadelphia at times and that he was still alive in 1883 at the age of eighty-six. The rest is silence.

CRITICISM

The few times George Moses Horton was acknowledged during the nineteenth century he was noticed in three different ways: one, by a poem or two published in a periodical, with either a simple identification of the poet, a plea for his freedom, or a brief account of his life taken from Horton's autobiography; two, by comments on Horton from those who knew him at the University of North Carolina; and three, by introductions to his volumes of verse by the editors or compilers. None of these commented on his poetry except for one sentence by Kemp Battle: "His poetry as a rule rhymes well, but may be classed with doggerel" (1888: 229).

In the first six decades of the twentieth century, Horton's poems, usually the same few from *The Hope of Liberty*, appeared in several anthologies and in brief articles about him derived entirely from Battle, Cobb, Weeks, and Horton's own words. The first extended criticism of his verse came from Vernon Loggins in 1931. Loggins ironically found echoes in this "primitive poetry" of "familiar Methodist hymns. . . . Pope, Byron, Tom Moore, Burns, and even Milton" (332, 116). Horton's verse, Loggins declared, was "imitative and affected," its imagery and rhythms a "hodgepodge"; and it was "carefree," showing that the poet was "intoxicated with his own cleverness" (111, 116, 110). Loggins dismissed Horton's art with a patronizing wave: "In Horton's grotesque music and bizarre imagination something which is foreign to the Caucasian mind is delightfully revealed" (117). In 1939, J. Saunders Redding gave Horton's verse a better but mixed review: Horton had the "audacity and color" lacking in Jupiter Hammon and the "enthusiasm and racial kinship" missing in Phillis Wheatley; he invested both emotion and thought in his verse, and he felt "something of the wonder and mystery, the tragic beauty, and the pathetic ugliness of life. Above all, he had the gift of laughter. He was the first 'natural-born' poet of the negro race in America" (13). Redding also said that Horton's antislavery poetry was selfish and conceited, and his historical importance "as the forerunner of the minstrel poets" outweighs "whatever of intrinsic poetical value his poems possess" (16, 18). Mattie Lakin's 1951 thesis, which remains unpublished and inaccessible to general readers, sympathetically surveyed Horton's verse, illustrated his use of varied forms and meters and imagery from everyday life and nature, and suggested influences on his poems from the Bible through Byron. Lakin claimed that although the poems were imitative and conventional, they had value as true and sincere reflections of Horton's personality and beliefs as well as of the times in which he lived.

The first (and only) book-length biography of Horton was *The Black Poet* (1966), in which Richard Walser combined "*in toto* the short autobiography" (vii) from *The Poetical Works*, introductions from other volumes, and Horton's poems and letters, along with data from North Carolina county records, United States Census reports, histories of North Carolina, and comments on Horton from books and periodicals to date. Walser interpreted, extended, and embroidered these data for a highly subjective account of Horton; *The Black Poet* is a potpourri of useful facts, apocrypha, and surmises which later writers repeat. Walser's evaluation of the poet and his work is surprisingly unsympathetic; negative and demeaning criticisms far outweigh and consistently undercut his few positive remarks. For example, Walser praised Horton's "determination to live and be the Poet, the man of letters," at which "he *was* reasonably successful" because he was willing "to submit his talents to those who could use them" (71). He commended Horton for issuing "the first poetic protest by any slave anywhere of his status [in *The Hope of Liberty*]" (41) but said "the book should have been better than it was"—its poems were uninspired, imitative, "humdrum," and confused (42). In the same vein, Walser judged poems in *The Poetical Works* "for the most part derivative and lofty," the only sincere ones being the "few indigenous poems [with] a gleam of humor" (68). And in *Naked Genius* he found "an unexpected ruggedness" and "clear evidence of rapid and indiscriminate writing, . . . no prosodic improvement over the earlier works, nor is there more maturity. Yet, as a whole, it is not without charm" (99). Walser's most egregious criticism fell on Horton's antislavery poems and on the man himself. Horton's bondage was "not so bad" as the poems imply and "had never cramped him"; "the condition of servitude was easily borne; it presented few problems. . . . life was hardly more confining than for any man free to act but held to the exigencies of providing for himself and others" (32, 33). Horton "was happy enough"; he did not find his bondage "overly tragic or oppressive. Under the system he flourished, as would not have been the case had he been free" (33, 70). Furthermore, Walser stated, from the late 1840s on, Horton no longer thought about freedom at all, "for he had as much liberty as his simple requirements demanded" (72). For this biographer, freedom meant nothing more to Horton than "new material for rhyming" (30); thus, "his slavery verses pulsate with no inner yearning. They sound as if he were writing what was expected of him," and most of them "are selfish and unimpassioned, philosophic rather than realistic" (38, 70). All in all, the entire value of Horton's antislavery verse for the southerner Walser was to show how tolerant the South was toward publication of such protest (41). Commenting on Horton's other verses, Walser stressed their imitativeness, "the ding-dong of Wesley's hymns" and "stilted measures and pompous epithets" of Thomson and Young (25). Horton's poems about prominent men "boosted his ego. . . . He became cocky, but careful to retain an unctuousness which he had found useful" (63).

The evidence of Horton's poems, prose, and activities soundly disproves Walser's harsher criticisms which may have derived from Walser's bias against Horton and others of his race that occasionally surfaces. Walser noted the poet's "patience and endurance," which were the virtues "of his race, . . . In them was he fortunately Negro" (71). He deemed Horton an "uncomplicated fellow" at the beginning of his narrative (32) and an honest man "of courtesy, humility, and good morals" at the book's end (103). This last verdict is astonishing, for throughout the biography Walser heaped only vituperation on his subject. The slave, he said, was an unenergetic loafer who drank, fished, and "looked forward to days long, prosperous, and pleasant" (51). At the university, Horton was a beggar, a drunkard, a "fatiguing and garrulous" peddler of the "sheerest drivel" to college boys (55, 58). Walser hurled these epithets at Horton: sycophant, poseur, buffoon, troubadour in motley, jubilant harlequin, egoist, opportunist, and braggart. He found "effrontry" in Horton's letter to Swain (77); "insolence and swagger" in his letter to Greeley (78); "presumption and arrogance" in his defense of American literature (73); and "the height of the jester, the final glorification of the motley" in his 1859 "Address" (84). It was seventy-three years after the poet's death that a biography appeared, but Horton would not be grateful to the North Carolinian Richard Walser, who all but destroyed the man's complex identity and poetic reputation.

Later writers drew on Walser's biographical materials, but they did not repeat his negative criticism. Three studies appeared in 1974: my chapter on Horton in *Invisible Poets* stresses his remarkable achievements and poetic strengths; Patricia Williams's thesis usefully compares and contrasts the social and political protest poetry of the English Romantics with ideas and verse of African Americans, including Horton; and Merle Richmond's 130-page "interpretive study" and evaluation, although admittedly colored by "inference and conjecture," is, with its excellent notes, the most complete and sympathetic treatment of Horton to date. Richmond successfully refutes many erroneous and contradictory assertions about Horton by previous critics and laments their "appropriation of him as a regional ornament of the ante-bellum South" (181–82). In contrast to Walser, for example, Richmond calls Horton's defense of American literature a "public protest [that] became an Emersonian call for recognition in general of native poetic genius" (193). And he says of Horton's poems that "a distinct human personality emerges from his verse, complex and contradictory and fudged at times, but an authentic personality that is self-assertive in its hopes and its commentary on the human condition, that possesses irony and wit, that is, on occasion, bold enough to break with convention" (182–83). By "uttering the first black poetic outcry against slavery," Richmond concludes, Horton is historically "an important figure in the tradition . . . of resistance to oppression, of refusal to acquiesce in a state of inferiority" (198).

Other studies of Horton's poetry that appeared in the 1970s and 1980s included two dissertations. William Carroll performed the major task of transcribing all the poems in *Naked Genius*, and a few from earlier volumes, indicating changes in diction, punctuation, and usage in poems from *The Poetical Works* that reappear in the later volume; neither of these two volumes has been reprinted in a modern edition. Carroll places the poems in twelve thematic categories and intelligently discusses some poems. Carroll later contributed an essay on Horton to the *Dictionary of Literary Biography*; this material is largely derived from works by earlier writers. Lonnell E. Johnson's dissertation also draws on previous writings for Horton's life and criticism, and he points out biblical elements in Horton's antislavery poems. Blyden Jackson's 1989 article surveys the criticism to date and describes Horton's poetry as "decidedly less crude" than Jupiter Hammon's and "more versatile, both in form and sense" than Phillis Wheatley's; it "displays an amazing range of interests and proficiencies which would have done credit to many people in Horton's day who were not in chattel bondage" (95). Jackson also credits Horton's "adroit pillorying of man in his relatively petty misdemeanors" and the occasional presence of multiple meanings in the poems (99). Two writers, Richard Walser in 1975 and Robin Brabham in 1987, discovered acrostics by Horton in manuscript collections. John L. Cobbs (1981) finds a "key to thematic unity" in Horton's *The Hope of Liberty*, the motif or metaphor of flight: the flight of souls, of lovers, of imagination, of birds in nature, of slaves to liberty. Flight is not only escape, but "in a more positive sense it expresses 'soaring'—release, ecstasy, creation, and freedom" (446–49). Cobbs's convincing analysis concludes that all of Horton's early poems are "filtered through the consciousness of his own bondage" and thereby express hope for freedom, for flight (449). In Horton's poem "The Slave," Sondra O'Neale (1981) locates a "veiled Biblical symbol" in the contrast of two brothers, one elected and one rejected by God, within three pairs of brothers, demonstrating that while God may prefer one group over another, all should be free and equal. Daniel Ford's (1982) close reading of "Division of an Estate" yields a fine thorough analysis; Ford writes that the poem was "years ahead of its time in its subtle ambiguities, its unusual structural progression, and in its curiously mixed religious outlook." He examines the natural, Christian, and cosmic imagery throughout the poem to arrive at the confluence of the slave auction and judgment day at the end.

To best understand Horton's poetry and his overall achievements, it is useful to compare his work to that of contemporary white and African American poets. J. Saunders Redding, the dean of African American literary critics, wrote that "American Negro literature, so called, is American literature in fact, and that American Negro literature cannot be lopped off from the main body of American literary expression without doing grave harm to both as complementary instruments of historical and social diagnosis and as the joint and articulated corpus of American experience."[41] Merle Richmond said that by virtue of his poetry Horton "belongs to the company of early American writers who, . . . found their idiom as well as their inspiration in the American environment" (193). Richard Walser, too, placed Horton among American poets, although grudgingly: "Scores of American poets among his contemporaries outshone him, and hundreds matched him" (70). Walser failed to note that among these hundreds, only Horton was a slave. Much has been written about the influences on Horton's art of Methodist hymns, the Bible, eighteenth-century British poets of the Graveyard and Romantic schools, and Americans like Bryant; but the main body of *all* nineteenth-century American poetry, including Horton's, was indebted to these sources and inspired by the American environment. In its subjects, form, language, and attitudes, Horton's verse closely resembles that of white poets of his time and place. Below are topics (in alphabetical order) found in *Wood-Notes* (1854), a two-volume anthology of poetry by white North Carolinians. Each topic is followed by some titles of Horton's poems on the same themes (in parentheses is the collection from which the poem comes*):

The Bible (Old and New Testaments): "Praise of Creation" and "On the Truth of the Saviour" (*HL*); "Reflections" (*PW*); "On Epiphany" (*NG*).

Death, fear it not, God's will be done: "Imploring to be Resigned at Death" (*PW*).

Death of a loved one: "On the Death of Rebecca" (*HL*); "Eulogy on the Death of a Sister" (*NG*).

Death of an infant, tribute: "On the Death of an Infant" (*HL*).

Life, its shortness; glory and treasure last but a day: "Man, a Torch" and "Reflections from the Flash of a Meteor" (*PW*); "The Close of Life" and "To the King of Macedonia" (*NG*).

Love of women: Mary, Kate, Eliza, Corinna, etc.; love of love: "To Eliza" and "Love" (*HL*); "To Catherine," "The Powers of Love," and "Early Affection" (*PW*).

Marriage: "Consequences of a Happy Marriage" (*HL*); "The Cheerless Condition of Bachelorship" (*NG*).

Nature analogous to man: man also fades, decays back into the earth, dies: "One Generation Passeth Away and Another Cometh" (*NG*).

Nature, beauties and wonders of the seasons: "On Spring," "On Summer," "On Winter" (*HL*); "Departing Summer" (*PW*).

Nature's grandeur, scene of wild romance generates new feelings: "The Hermit's View from the Mountain" (*NG*).

Nature teaches morals, life's bright and dark sides: "The Rising Sun," "The Setting Sun" (*PW*).

*These abbreviations will be used in the following list and throughout the text: *HL*: *The Hope of Liberty*; *PW*: *The Poetical Works*; *NG*: *Naked Genius*.

Nostalgia, memories of youth, lost love, home: "The Traveller" and "Memory" (*PW*); "The Southern Refugee," "Fare thee Well, But Not Forever," "Regretted Past Time," and "The Friends Left at Home" (*NG*).

Poetry and fancy, tributes to: "On the Poetic Muse" (*HL*); "The Art of a Poet" and "To the Muse" (*NG*).

Soldiers off to fight, long for home, go bravely to battle: "The Thought of Home in Battle" and "The Soldier's Thought of Home" (*NG*).

Temperance Society, tribute: "The Intemperance Club" (*NG*).

Several poets in *Wood-Notes* use Horton's favorite image of flight, with many identical details and meanings: their poems summon mankind to fly, to soar like a bird from lust, sin, and death to purity, light, and love above; a "heart fettered in chains" seeks freedom, and love soars "with pinion unfurled"; the "music of heaven flies on wings"; shadows "fly down the sky on pinions"; the poetic spirit soars above nature. In Horton's "Heavenly Love," "pilgrim's spirits . . . soar on high" from sin to God's love, and the soul is summoned to "wing thy swift flight beyond the sun." In "On the Silence of a Young Lady," a lament for lost love, begins: "Oh, heartless dove! mount in the skies, / Spread thy soft wing upon the gale, / Or on thy sacred pinions rise, / Nor brood with silence in the vale." In "On the Poetic Muse" the poet soars "far above this world, . . . Aerial regions to explore"; "My towering thoughts with pinions rise," and the muse with "vivid flight . . . mounts on high" far above nature.

In his three volumes Horton used all the traditional "white" verse forms: heroic couplet; ballad with refrain; common, long, and short hymn meters; heroic quatrain; six-, seven-, and eight-line stanzas in single or combined meters—iambic, anapestic, trochaic, dactylic—with varied numbers of feet and rhyme schemes; and blank verse. He also employed classic image sequences of day to night and youth to old age, as well as internal refrains and patterns of questions and answers. Finally, Horton shared with his contemporaries the flaws of nineteenth-century poetry: intellectual and emotional banality, sentimentality, diffuseness, abstract and archaic diction, the pathetic fallacy, and excessive use of mythological-literary-biblical allusions.

In sum, the majority of Horton's verses seem indistinguishable from verse by white North Carolinians of his time who shared his environment and influences. He was a slave but always looked beyond slave culture to the white community for his role models and literary values. Horton lived in Chapel Hill's academic setting for half a century; he read the same books, from the Bible to Byron, and imbibed the same philosophic ideas and aesthetic standards as the white poets; he wrote poetry to please a white audience, the university professors and students who were the only possible buyers of his books. Yet there are qualities in some of Horton's poetry that clearly set his work apart from that of both his white and African American contemporaries.

Among the major African American poets of the century, only a few published before the Civil War, and all of them were free-born, living in the North. Their finest work was militant protest poetry that explicitly attacked government, church, laws, and evils of slavery and demanded emancipation and racial justice. Horton's antislavery verse is unlike theirs: a slave who wished to write and publish in the South (both illegal activities) could not realistically hurl anathemas on proslavery institutions or portray blood-curdling details of rack and whip and perilous escapes. Forbidden to him even more than the subjects was the free poets' tone of anguished despair, vengeful fury, righteous indignation, or bitter mockery, coupled with passionate race pride. Only one Horton poem, "The Slave" (1865), written when he was a free man, approached the militancy of early black protest poetry.

Horton wrote eleven poems concerned entirely with slavery and freedom; another dozen mentioned the bondslave, confinement, and liberty; and several poems, ostensibly on other topics, may be read as allegorical musings on his own bondage, for example, hope ("To Miss Tempe"); the art of poetry ("George Moses Horton, Myself"); death ("Death of a Favorite"); a horse ("Death of an Old Carriage Horse"). It is in these poems of bondage and liberty and others related to them in their patterns of imagery that Horton's work is unique and most distinguished. In his early poems, the best ones, he laments *his* bondage and pleads for *his* liberty; the speaker, the "I," is unmistakenly poet Horton, whose personal confinement vies with longed-for freedom; but the very presence of the poem denies its assertion that physical freedom is essential to write poetry, and both the tension and its negation give the poems their power. In later antislavery poems like "The Slave's Reflection" and "Slavery" (both 1865) the third-person speaker's crafted generalized sentiments are distanced from both the poet and reality. A second unique quality of some antislavery poems is their reliance on an intellectual argument: in cool, reasonable, and high poetic language, the poet bases his pleas for freedom on the philosophical principle of Thomas Jefferson's *Declaration* (1776) that "the laws of nature and of nature's God" confer on all men "inalienable rights" to "life, liberty, and the pursuit of happiness." In Horton's "On Liberty and Slavery" (*HL*), the slave is "deprived of all created bliss" and of "liberty" and craves the "sacred sun" of liberty, "the gift of nature's God," to rise. Horton later expressed the same view in his "Address," when he said he had always been opposed to monarchy, "for I know that liberty is undoubtedly the birth right which heaven has conferred upon the world of mankind" (28). Similar sentiments mark "The Slave" (1865), where eight of ten stanzas ask slaveholders by what "right divine," what "lawful right" do they violate the "golden rule of Heaven," the laws of "sovereign justice" that "robbed him of his birthright—Liberty." God will defend the "sacred right of nature" and will restore "the right" by abolishing slavery. By evoking the sacred words of Jefferson, Horton asserted his (and later, the race's) right to citizenship as a learned and patriotic American, a disciple of the beloved Virginian. Evidence from other poems shows that he truly embraced the idea of natural rights. Horton's verses on nature, poetry-making, and religion depart from traditional white approaches to the subjects and are related to his antislavery verse by their stress on a single theme: liberty—physical, emotional, and mental—is the law of nature, the poet's Muse, and the law and spirit of God. The poet's devout desire for liberty, explicit or implied, unifies his work and proves that however benign his bondage seemed, to Horton slavery was onerous, unnatural, and hateful. And his hope of liberty never flagged; in his "Address" of 1859, he said: "The privation of liberty brutalizes human intellect, dulls the enterprizing [*sic*] spirit into timidity and confusion; it is a death blow to the pleasures of human life" (29).

Horton presents his characteristic theme almost formulaically; for example, in "Lines, . . ." (*HL*), the poet's sacred muse = benign nature = voices of the saved = the coming of Spring = loving marriage = music = manumission = eternal Providence. In his religious verses, the spirit is imprisoned not by sin and nature but by slavery's chains; Christ is not a bloody slaughtered lamb but the tree of life and tree of liberty. In "Heavenly Love" (*HL*) God's grace "can ransom every slave." In "On the Truth of the Saviour" (*HL*) the powers of Jesus to calm the seas, drive off "plagues," heal mankind, and raise the dead match the powers of liberty in "The Slave's Complaint" (*HL*), where hope of liberty wakes the dead and heals the lame and blind. Elsewhere Horton presents faith, God, and death as natural extensions of life, allied to poetry and freedom. In "Praise of Creation" (*HL*) he gracefully synthesizes simple piety, poetic aspiration, and love of nature: a poet speaker describes the creation of the world accompanied by music (stanzas 1–7); he summons nature—eagles, lions, thunders, mountains, netherworlds, volcanoes, oceans, cataracts—to join the "universal concert" of praise and bids his "muse" join in (stanzas 8–13); but his "weary muse delays" and his soul floats along on the music.

Horton develops variations on the central contrast between liberty and bondage in poems on many topics, using concrete and emotive terms. Liberty is a cheerful sound or music, a singing dove upon whose wings the slave rides, a golden prize, a nurturing mother, a sheltering tree, the bright sun, sweet perfume, spring, God's spirit, beams of light, heat of flames, heights, dawn and morning, love, and hope. Liberty is sacred, blessed, heavenly, calm, joyful, and peaceful. And Liberty smiles, coos, sings, and soars or ascends. In contrast, bondage is chains, storms, rocks, winter, clouds, ocean billows, night, a maze, a thief. Bondage is haggard, barbaric, tyrannous, fearful, despairing, dreary, groping, vile, sordid, gloomy, cruel, and loathsome. Bondage thunders and roars, rages, darkens, drowns, imprisons, and kills. These contrasting image patterns personalize Horton's verse from 1829 to 1865 and reveal that what he loved and desired—liberty, nature, the muse of poetry, and the spirit of God—were inseparable. Paradoxically, while he begged for liberty in order to write poetry, Horton wrote his best poems, those collected in the 1829 and 1845 volumes, while he was a slave. Slavery did not inhibit Horton's talent; rather, it forced his "fettered genius" to articulate his goal, Liberty, and to embrace all his experiences in a unified vision which he communicated in an impassioned figurative vocabulary.

A pair of verses on poetry-writing suggests one change in Horton's art when he at last gained his freedom. In "On the Poetic Muse" (*HL*) the poet is a Romantic: he recollects in tranquility; then his muse flies through "mental skies" to "wonders" far above nature, to "scenes remote . . . as never yet exprest." In "The Art of the Poet" (*NG*), however, a neoclassical caution slips in, as the poet concedes that "nature first inspires the man," but he must then "mark well every rule," refine and polish his verse for "its glory bright to show." For the most part, Horton's verse in 1865 lost its spontaneity, freshness, particularity, and sense of wonder. Much of the weakness of poems in *Naked Genius* can be blamed on their hasty composition—Horton scribbled ninety new poems in a few months while trudging the roads with the Union army. And the poet was almost seventy years old. Instead of hope of transcendence and joy at the bounties of creation, the poems preached the transience of life and the need for moral behavior; they comment on current events and heroes and lament losses and loneliness. The first few lines of "George Moses Horton, Myself," which opens *Naked Genius*, sets the tone and suggests the problem of the volume as a whole:

> I feel myself in need
> Of the inspiring strains of ancient lore,
> My heart to lift, my empty mind to feed,
> And all the world explore.

The poet has lost his inspiration; his genius, confined since boyhood, still yearns to soar, but it is now shackled to an old man's mind and body. Horton's awareness of his age, his sense of lost opportunity and artistic failure, and his dogged reiteration of forty-year-old sentiments comprise a message of despair, of hopelessness barely hidden by the brave words.

Most poems of 1865 have biographical interest but small literary value. Horton's philosophical musings on life and death are not original, but in "The Close of Life" (*NG*) we can see him shrug a cocksure shoulder as he chants, "I'm here today, but gone to-morrow, / To my long repose." He does not fear death, and in several poems he accepts that all is vanity, and all men, low and highborn, must die; therefore, it is foolish to pursue transient beauty, fame, power, or riches. Whether these ideas are "sour grapes" or a true change of heart, the question remains, how then should a man live? The poems of Horton's late years recommend prudence, self-control, study, self-reliance, and work with ease—he never advocated hard labor. The poet warns against idle chatter, empty leisure, pride, extravagance, drink, giving or taking charity, stealing, gambling, and wandering. Horton addressed this list of virtues and vices mainly to the freed slaves in 1865. His advice strikingly anticipates the preaching of African American poets in the last three decades of the nineteenth century, poets such as Daniel Webster Davis and Joseph S. Cotter Sr., who were drawn into the orbit of Booker T. Washington. In fact, after the Civil War, when militant protest poetry died, all black poets struggled to justify to white society their race's talents and capacities for citizenship by embracing poetic themes, techniques, and attitudes of their white contemporaries, very much as Horton did decades before. Later black poetry was also uplifting, like Horton's "Rosabella"; sentimental, like his love ditties; and integrationist, like "The Union of Parties." Although Horton's later work suffered from hackneyed language, confusion of topics and tones, and tired, generic sentiments, a handful are vintage Horton: the powerful antislavery poem, "The Slave," with its unforgettable image of the brood-sow's black and "sandy colored pigs"; the rollicking "Snaps for Dinner, Snaps for Breakfast and Snaps for Lunch," that puns satirically on "snaps"; two clever satires of Jefferson Davis, "Jefferson in a Tight Place" and "Davis' Flight"; and the sincerely devotional "Rosabella," with its ringing refrain.

Two other categories of Horton's verse are the poems of love and misogyny and the "folk" verse. His earliest works, which he had been selling to students for over ten years before *The Hope of Liberty* appeared, were acrostics and verses praising ladies' charms, bemoaning their obstinacy, or bidding them farewell. The best of his love poems share merits of rhythmic repetition, melodious phrasing, and elegantly simple language. But by 1829, such verses had become formulaic, and except for a few such as "Love" (*HL*) and "Early Affection" (*PW*), they share hyperbolic and abstract sentiments, clichéd and bombastic diction, obscure allusions, and garbled thought. The power of love, however, remained strong for Horton through the 1865 poems: Love could raise the poor and weary, shelter the homeless, free the captive, mend marriages, and unify the nation. But Horton also wrote some ten poems opposing the paeans to love, almost all in *Naked Genius*. They depict women and wives as treacherous, greedy, disloyal shrews, and jailers of men. Love in these poems is a snare that beguiles and deceives, and deprives man of his freedom and his manhood. Although hard evidence is lacking, such poems suggest that Horton's love life was none too joyous between 1845 and 1865.

Finally, Horton wrote several earthy verses on daily activities, which were invigorated by colloquial diction, homely detail, a hearty spirit, wry wit, and acute observation. These are "folk" verses by virtue of their everyday subjects and occasional ballad forms; but they do not conform to the oral folkloristic and melodramatic traditions of slave narratives, nor African elements of southern slave culture, nor the minstrel and plantation stereotypes of later dialect verse. Several pieces hide a serious intent beneath a jolly surface. For example, "The Creditor to His Proud Debtor" (*HL*) presents two messages under its lively ballad rhythms, taunting tone, and whimsical refrain: money is the root of all evil and neither a borrower nor a lender be. "The Tippler to His Bottle" (*PW*) and "The Woodman and Money Hunter" (*PW*) similarly moralize against drinking and money-hunting respectively, vices in which Horton indulged, but the lessons are sugar-coated with musical meters, easy rhymes, and "story" lines. Such poems disclose Horton grappling with temptation and need but artfully rising above them with folksy detail and self-deprecating humor. In other "folk" verses, Horton mourns two horses, one worked to death and one stolen; and "Troubled with the Itch" (*PW*), surely his most physically painful confessions, uniquely describes a skin disease and stinking salve.

Horton's three volumes of poetry cover a wide range of subjects, presented in a variety of styles and voices. But the strongest voice is that of the slave who for sixty-eight years lived mainly in a white world whose culture he longed to share. All his life, Horton struggled for literacy to write poetry; he begged for manumission to write poetry; he earned modest freedom of movement and a livelihood by writing poetry; he published three volumes, and although all failed to bring him freedom or profit, it was this struggle to burst his chains and gain liberty, learning, and respect from the white community that galvanized Horton's art. At the end of his life he was pleased to be called "Poet."

EDITORIAL NOTE

Spelling and punctuation in the poems reproduced in this volume are Horton's. The material in brackets has been added by the editor.

NOTES

1. Unless otherwise noted, all quotations are from Horton's autobiographical sketch in *The Poetical Works* (1845). Information about William Horton, his family, and their farms are from Walser, *The Black Poet.*

2. "An Address. The Stream of Liberty and Science. To Collegiates of the University of N.C. By George M. Horton The Black Bard." Hereafter cited in the text as "Address."

3. Johnson, *Ante-Bellum North Carolina*, 569–70.

4. Hilty, *Toward Freedom For All*, 42–55 passim.

5. Ibid., 93–96.

6. Parker, *Running For Freedom*, 9, 10–11, 21–22.

7. W. D. Williamson, quoted in Henderson, *The Campus*, 22.

8. UNC in 1830 had only 80 students, down from a high of 173 in 1823; a staff of seven; land worth some $160,000; debts of about $20,000, and an operating deficit of $7,007.47. By contrast, in the same year, seventy-year-old Harvard University had 6,000 students, 500 teachers, and property worth $15 million (Battle, *History of the University of North Carolina*, 326–29, 377, 390).

9. Walser, *Black Poet*, 20.

10. Battle, *History of the University of North Carolina*, 298–99, 452–54, 464–65, 573–85, 619.

11. Johnson, *Ante-Bellum North Carolina*, 212.

12. *Grandfather's Tales*, 212.

13. *History of the University of North Carolina*, 601–7.

14. Ibid., 435, 645, 703.

15. *Grandfather's Tales*, 212.

16. "George Horton, The Slave Poet," 229; Battle, *History of the University of North Carolina*, 603.

17. James Henderson, son of Major Pleasant Henderson, was an 1806 graduate of UNC and a practicing physician in Chapel Hill in the 1820s during Horton's first manumission campaign.

18. Battle, *History of the University of North Carolina*, 344–45.

19. Ibid., 608, 611; Henderson, *The Campus of the First State University*, 46.

20. In his 1888 article, Kemp Battle published two verses by Horton that were "found among the papers of Professor Graves's father." Horton wrote the verses "in return for some kindness done him by Mr. Graves" ("George Horton, The Slave Poet," 230). The "father" Battle refers to was Ralph Henry Graves Sr., an 1826 graduate of UNC and tutor in mathematics until 1844; the junior Graves who found the verses was a sophomore at UNC in 1868 and later a professor at the university. It was Stephen Weeks who identified "G" as "possibly Professor William Mercer Green" ("George Moses Horton: Slave Poet," 577). Green, who graduated with the class of 1818, was professor of rhetoric and logic (1836–49) and chaplain of the university (1838–49); he left Chapel Hill in 1849 to become Protestant Episcopal Bishop of Mississippi. Based on this evidence, it seems more likely that "G" was Ralph Henry Graves Sr.

21. "A North Carolina Poet," 510.

22. Letter to Paltsits. The manuscript Cobb refers to may be Horton's "Address. The Stream of Liberty and Science" because its title page says: "Presented to the Library of the University of North Carolina by Collier Cobb."

23. Battle, "George Horton, The Slave Poet," 230; Weeks, "George Moses Horton," 576.

24. Walser, *Black Poet*, 60.

25. Aptheker, *American Negro Slave Revolts*, 309–10.

26. From the Raleigh *Register*, October 13, 1831; quoted in Johnson, *Ante-Bellum North Carolina*, 573.

27. Connor, *North Carolina*, 2:24–26; quoted in Lefler, *North Carolina History*, 153.

28. Johnson, *Ante-Bellum North Carolina*, 55, 476.

29. Quoted in Lefler, *North Carolina History*, 275–76.

30. Connor, *North Carolina*, 2:119.

31. Battle, *History of the University of North Carolina*, 654–57; Connor, *North Carolina*, 2:121–22.

32. Battle, *History of the University of North Carolina*, 425, 534.

33. Ibid., 603–4. Concerning Horton's complexion, Weeks wrote that people in Chapel Hill knew him "as a full-blooded Negro who boasted of the purity of his black blood," but "Negroes who knew him in Philadelphia report that he was of mixed blood" ("George Moses Horton: Slave Poet," 571–72).

34. "Diary of Thomas Miles Garrett," 242–43.

35. Quoted in Richmond, *Bid the Vassal Soar*, 191–92.

36. Battle, *History of the University of North Carolina*, 719–37 passim.

37. Weeks, "George Moses Horton: Slave Poet," 576.

38. Letter to Paltsits.

39. Presented September 24, 1886, to the Southern Students of Harvard College; published as "An American Man of Letters in the *University of North Carolina Magazine* and also in *The North Carolina Review*, October 3, 1909.

40. *Bid the Vassal Soar*, 173–74. Richmond consulted the periodical archives of the Philadelphia Free Library; the University of Pennsylvania; Haverford College; the Pennsylvania Historical Society; and the Library Company of Philadelphia and found no reference to any work by Horton (*Bid the Vassal Soar*, 208 n).

41. "Negro Writing in America," 8.

Bibliography

WORKS BY GEORGE MOSES HORTON

Books

The Hope of Liberty. Containing a Number of Poetical Pieces. Raleigh: J. Gales & Son, 1829. 22 pp. 21 poems.

Poems by a Slave. 2nd ed. Philadelphia: Lewis Gunn, 1837. 23 pp. 21 poems, the same as those in *The Hope of Liberty.*

Memoir and Poems of Phillis Wheatley, a Native African and a Slave. Also, Poems by a Slave. 3rd ed. Boston: Isaac Knapp, 1838. 155 pp. 21 poems by Horton, the same as those in *The Hope of Liberty.*

The Poetical Works. Hillsborough, N.C.: D. Heartt, 1845. 99 pp. 44 poems.

Naked Genius. Raleigh: Wm. B. Smith & Co., Southern Field and Fireside Book Publishing House, 1865. 160 pp. 132 poems (90 new).

Periodicals (Uncollected)

"Lines to My ——." *Southern Literary Messenger* (April 1843): 238.

"Slavery. By a Carolinian Slave named George Horton." *Freedom's Journal* (July 18, 1828).

———. *Liberator* (March 29, 1834).

"What is Time." *Chapel Hill Weekly Gazette,* May 9, 1857.

Prose Manuscripts

"An Address. The Stream of Liberty and Science. To Collegiates of the University of N.C. By George M. Horton The Black Bard." 1859. North Carolina Collection, University of North Carolina, Chapel Hill. 29 pp.

*Letter to Garrison (1844), *letter to Greeley (1852), and *two letters to Swain (neither dated). David Lowry Swain Papers, Southern Historical Collection, University of North Carolina, Chapel Hill.

Poetry Manuscripts

Gillespie and Wright Family Papers, Southern Historical Collection, University of North Carolina, Chapel Hill

*Manuscripts marked by an asterisk are in Horton's handwriting

"An acrostic by George Horton [LUCY G. WRIGHT]"; "An acrostic by George Horton the negro bard [JANE E. MCIVER]," n.d.

Pettigrew Family Papers, Southern Historical Collection, University of North Carolina, Chapel Hill

*"An acrostic on the pleasures of beauty [JULIA SHEPARD]," ca. 1835

"The Emigrant Girl"; "On Ghosts"; "An Acrostic, Mr. Davenport's address to his lady [DOCTRINE DAVENPORT / MDD]"; "His lady's reply [MARY M. DAVENPORT / DD]"; "An Acrostic To their little daughter [MARY PETTIGREW DAVENPORT / DM]," written for William Shepard Pettigrew, ca. 1836

Simpson-Biddle-Carraway Papers, North Carolina Division of Archives and History, Raleigh

"Acrostics [2 stanzas: MARY E. V. POWELL; SION HART ROGERS]." A note on the reverse reads: "An accrostic [*sic*] Written by a Negro, at Chapel Hill," ca. 1844.

David Lowry Swain Papers, Southern Historical Collection, University of North Carolina, Chapel Hill

*"The Poet's Feeble Petition," on reverse of Horton's letter to Horace Greeley, September 11, 1852

Torrance-Banks Family Papers, University of North Carolina at Charlotte Library

*"Inimitable beauty, An acrostic to [SOPHIA ALEXANDER]"

*"For the fair Miss M. M. McL[ean] An acrostic [MARY MCLEAN and fifteen additional lines]"; after last line, "Mr Torence"; a note on this page states: "Written by the Negroe [*sic*] Poet of Chapel Hill about 1853–4 or 5"

REFERENCE WORKS

History

Aptheker, Herbert. *American Negro Slave Revolts.* New ed. New York: International Publications, 1969.

Bassett, John Spencer. *Slavery in the State of North Carolina.* Johns Hopkins University Studies in Historical and Political Science, ed. Herbert B. Adams, series 17, no. 7–8. Baltimore: Johns Hopkins Press, 1899.

Battle, Kemp P. *History of the University of North Carolina from Its Beginning to the Death of President Swain, 1789–1868.* Vol. 1. Raleigh: Edwards & Broughton, 1907.

Blassingame, John W. *The Slave Community: Plantation Life in the Antebellum South.* 2nd ed. New York: Oxford University Press, 1979.

Caldwell, Wallace E. "The Humanities at the University of North Carolina, 1795–1945, A Historical Survey." In *A State University Surveys the Humanities,* edited by Loren C. MacKinney, et al., 3–30. Chapel Hill: University of North Carolina Press, 1945.

Censer, Jane Turner. *North Carolina Planters and Their Children, 1800–1860.* Baton Rouge: Louisiana State University Press, 1984.

Connor, R[obert] D[iggs] W[imberly]. *North Carolina: Rebuilding an Ancient Commonwealth, 1584–1925.* 4 vols. Chicago: American Historical Society, 1929. 2 vols. Spartanburg, S.C.: Reprint Co., 1973.

Creecy, Richard Benbury. *Grandfather's Tales of North Carolina History.* Raleigh: Edwards & Broughton, 1901.

Henderson, Archibald. *The Campus of the First State University.* Chapel Hill: University of North Carolina Press, 1949.

Hilty, Hiram H. *Toward Freedom For All: North Carolina Quakers and Slavery.* Richmond, Indiana: Friends United Press, 1984.

Johnson, Guion Griffis. *Ante-Bellum North Carolina: A Social History.* Chapel Hill: University of North Carolina Press, 1937.

Lefler, Hugh Talmage. *North Carolina History Told By Contemporaries.* 4th ed., rev. and enl. Chapel Hill: University of North Carolina Press, 1965.

Parker, Freddie L. *Running For Freedom: Slave Runaways in North Carolina, 1775–1840.* New York: Garland, 1993.

Spencer, Cornelia Phillips. *The Last Ninety Days of the War in North-Carolina.* New York: Watchman Publications, 1866.

Stamp, Kenneth M. *The Peculiar Institution: Slavery in the Ante-Bellum South.* New York: Random House, 1956.

Yearns, W. Buck, and John G. Barrett, eds. *North Carolina Civil War Documentary.* Chapel Hill: University of North Carolina Press, 1980.

Criticism and Biography

Adams, Raymond. "North Carolina's Pioneer Negro Poet." Greensboro [N.C.] *Daily News,* November 24, 1929, sec. 2, p. B5.

Battle, Kemp P. "George Horton, The Slave Poet." *The University [of North Carolina] Magazine* 7 (May 1888): 229–32.

Brabham, Robin. "To the 'Tip-Top Belles' of Mecklenburg County: Two Acrostics by George Moses Horton." *College Language Association Journal* 30 (June 1987): 454–60.
Brawley, Benjamin. "George Moses Horton." In *Early Negro American Writers.* , 110–22. Chapel Hill: University of North Carolina Press, 1935.
Carroll, William. "George Moses Horton (1797?–1883?)." *Dictionary of Literary Biography*. Vol. 50. 1986, 190–201.
———. "Naked Genius: The Poetry of George Moses Horton, Slave Bard of North Carolina, 1797?-1883?." Ph.D. diss., University of North Carolina, 1977.
Carruth, Hayden. "Self-Taught Slave Found How to Make Poetry Pay." *The News and Observer* [Raleigh], November 30, 1941, p. 4.
Child, L. Maria. "The Slave Poet." *The Freedman's Book*, 111–13. Boston: Ticknor and Fields, 1865.
Clarke, Mary Bayard (Tenella), comp. *Wood-Notes; or, Carolina Carols: A Collection of North Carolina Poetry*. 2 vols. Raleigh: Warren L. Pomeroy, 1854.
Cobb, Collier. "An American Man of Letters." *University of North Carolina Magazine*, o.s., 40, n.s., 27 (October 1909) 25–32. Presented as a paper at Harvard University, September 23, 1886. Also printed in *The North Carolina Review*, October 3, 1909.
———. Letter to Victor Hugo Paltsits, January 10, 1929. Clipping File, Manuscripts, Archives and Rare Books Division. Schomburg Center for Research in Black Culture. The New York Public Library. Astor, Lenox and Tilden Foundations.
Cobbs, John L. "George Moses Horton's *Hope of Liberty*: Thematic Unity in Early American Black Poetry." *College Language Association Journal* 24 (June 1981): 441–50.
Cullen, Countee. "The Dark Tower." *Opportunity* 5 (June 1927): 180–81.
Farrison, W. Edward. "George Moses Horton: Poet for Freedom." *College Language Association Journal* 14 (March 1971): 227–41.
Ford, Daniel G. "Comments on George Moses Horton's 'Division of an Estate.'" *Publications of the Arkansas Philological Association* 8 (Fall 1982): 1–8.
"From the *Child's Friend* [Boston, September 1845] 'The Slave Poet.'" *National Anti-Slavery Standard* (May 28, 1846): 208.
Garrett, Thomas Miles. "Diary of Thomas Miles Garrett at the

University of North Carolina, 1849." Part 1. ed. John Bowen Hamilton. *North Carolina Historical Review* 38 (April 1961): 241–62.

"George M. Horton." *Freedom's Journal* (August 29, September 12, October 3, 1828).

Jackson, Blyden. "George Moses Horton and David Walker." In *A History of Afro-American Literature: The Long Beginning, 1746–1895*, 83–102. Baton Rouge: Louisiana State University Press, 1989.

———. "George Moses Horton, North Carolinian." *North Carolina Historical Review* 53 (April 1976): 140–47.

Johnson, Lonnell E. "Portrait of the Bondslave in the Bible: Slavery and Freedom in the Works of Four Afro-American Poets." Ph.D. diss., Indiana University, 1986.

Lakin, Mattie Temple Tatum. "George Moses Horton." M.A. thesis, North Carolina College at Durham, 1951.

Levine, Lawrence W. *Black Culture and Black Consciousness: Afro-American Folk Thought from Slavery to Freedom.* New York: Oxford University Press, 1977.

Loggins, Vernon. "Chapter III." In *The Negro Author: His Development in America to 1900*, 107–17 et passim. New York: Columbia University Press, 1931.

Manning, Bernard L. *The Hymns of Wesley and Watts.* London: Epworth Press, 1942.

"A North Carolina Poet" [with poem, "Good-Bye"]. *University of North Carolina Magazine* 9 (April 1860): 510.

Oldham, Edward A. "North Carolina Poets, Past and Present." *North Carolina Poetry Review* 2 (January–February 1935): 77–80.

O'Neale, Sondra. "Roots of Our Literary Culture: George Moses Horton and Biblical Protest." *Obsidian* 7 (1981): 18–28.

Redding, J. Saunders. "The Forerunners." In *To Make a Poet Black*, 13–18. Chapel Hill: University of North Carolina Press, 1939.

———. "Negro Writing in America." *The New Leader* 43 (May 16, 1960): 8.

Richmond, Merle A. *Bid the Vassal Soar: Interpretative Essays on the Life and Poetry of Phillis Wheatley (ca. 1753–1784) and George Moses Horton (ca. 1797–1883)*, 81–198. Washington: Howard University Press, 1974.

Sherman, Joan R. "George Moses Horton." In *Invisible Poets: Afro-*

Americans of the Nineteenth Century. 2nd ed., 5–19. Urbana: University of Illinois Press, 1989.
"Three Negro Poets: Horton, Mrs. Harper, and Whitman." *Journal of Negro History* 2 (October 1917): 384–92.
Walser, Richard. *The Black Poet: being the remarkable story (partly told my [*sic*] himself) of George Moses Horton a North Carolina slave*. New York: Philosophical Library, 1966.
———. "Newly Discovered Acrostic by George Moses Horton." *College Language Association Journal* 19 (December 1975): 258–60.
Weeks, Stephen B. "George Moses Horton: Slave Poet." *Southern Workman* 43 (October 1914): 571–77.
Williams, Patricia Ann Robinson. "Poets of Freedom: The English Romantics and Early Nineteenth-Century Black Poets." Ph.D. diss., University of Illinois, 1974.

Uncollected Poems

EXCITED FROM READING THE OBEDIENCE OF NATURE TO HER LORD IN THE VESSEL ON THE SEA

Master, we perish if thou sleep,
We know not whence to fly;
The thunder seems to rock the deep,
Death frowns from all the sky.

He rose, he ran, and looking out,
He said, ye seas, be still;
What art thou, cruel storm, about?
All silenced at his will.

Dost thou not know that thou art mine,
And all thy liquid stores;
Who ordered first the sun to shine
And gild thy swelling shores.

My smile is but the death of harm,
Whilst riding on the wind,
My power restrains the thunder's arm,
Which dies in chains confined.

ca. 1820s;
quoted by Horton in his autobiography, *The Poetical Works*, 1845

SLAVERY

By a Carolinian Slave named George Horton

When first my bosom glowed with hope,
I gaz'd as from a mountain top
On some delightful plain;
But oh! how transient was the scene—
It fled as though it had not been,
And all my hopes were vain.

How oft this tantalizing blaze
Has led me through deception's maze;
My friend became my foe—
Then like a plaintive dove I mourn'd,
To bitter all my sweets were turn'd,
And tears began to flow.

Why was the dawning of my birth
Upon this vile accursed earth,
Which is but pain to me?
Oh! that my soul had winged its flight,
When first I saw the morning light,
To worlds of liberty!

Come melting Pity from afar
And break this vast, enormous bar
Between a wretch and thee;
Purchase a few short days of time,
And bid a vassal rise sublime
On wings of liberty.

Is it because my skin is black,
That thou should'st be so dull and slack,
And scorn to set me free?
Then let me hasten to the grave,
The only refuge for the slave,
Who mourns for liberty.

The wicked cease from trouble there;
No more I'd languish or despair—
        The weary there can rest.
Oppression's voice is heard no more,
Drudg'ry and pain, and toil are o'er.
        Yes! there I shall be blest.

Freedom's Journal, July 18, 1828
Liberator, March 29, 1834

GRATITUDE

By G. M. Horton

Dedicated to the Gentlemen [sic] who takes so kind an interest in his behalf

Joy kindles by thy vital gale,
And breathes true philanthropy;
Thus with delight I hail
The dawn of Liberty.

The song of Gratitude I owe
To thee from whom these pleasures rise,
And strains of praise to thee shall flow,
Until my memory dies.

Far from this dark inclement place
Unto thy sacred beams I'll flee;
Unto the soothing smiles of grace,
The smiles of liberty.

Enraptur'd by the pleasing charm,
Aloud will I my joys proclaim;
And soar above oppression's storm,
And triumph in thy name.

Philanthropy, thou feeling dove,
Whose voice can sound the vassal free,
Upon thy wing of humane love
I'll fly to liberty.

Through inclement seas distress'd,
Where all the storms of hardship roar.
Ere long I humbly hope to rest,
On freedom's peaceful shore.

May Providence reward each man
Who feels such safe regard for me,
And in his breast enroll a plan
Devis'd for liberty.

May all the smiles of heaven attend
Thy life who thus relieves the poor,
And showers of blessings down descend
To amplify thy store.

Thus may thy feeling heart rejoice,
And cause me to rejoice with thee,
And triumph with a cheerful voice,
The voice of liberty.

Freedom's Journal, September 5, 1828

LINES TO MY ——

I would be thine when morning breaks
    On my enraptured view;
When every star her tow'r forsakes,
And every tuneful bird awakes,
    And bids the night adieu.
I would be thine, when Phœbus speeds
    His chariot up the sky,
Or on the heel of night he treads,
And thro' the heav'n's refulgence spreads—
    Thine would I live or die.
I would be thine, thou fairest one,
    And hold thee as my boon,
When full the morning's race is run,
And half the fleeting day is gone,
    Thine let me rest at noon.
I would be thine when ev'ning's veil
    O'er-mantles all the plain,
When Cynthia smiles on every dale,
And spreads like thee, her nightly sail
    To dim the starry train.
Let me be thine, altho' I take
    My exit from this world;
And when the heavens with thunder shake,
And all the wheels of time shall break,
    With globes to nothing hurl'd,
        I would be thine.

Southern Literary Messenger, April 1843

Mistress of green in flowers arrayed
Alluring all my heart away
Replete with glory not to fade
Yet flourish in eternal May—
Eternalized by distant fame—
Void of a shade in bloom divine—
Pleasures await thy sacred name
Or bid thee still proceed (s) to shine
Who has surpassed thy heavenly mein
Expression will forbear to tell
Like thee not one I yet have seen
Let all adore *thee* lovely belle

So let our names togather blend
In floods of union to the end
Or flow togather soul in soul
Nor distance break the soft control—
How pleasing is the thought to me
A thought of such a nymph as thee
Reverts my language into song
That flows delightful soft along—
Return to me a soft reply
On which I must with joy rely
Give me thy hand and then thy heart
Entirely mingled not to part
Relume the tapor near expired
Seeking a friend so long desired—

ca. 1844

THE POET'S FEEBLE PETITION

Bewailing mid the ruthless wave,
 I lift my feeble hand to thee.
Let me no longer live a slave
 But drop these fetters and be free.

Why will regardless fortune sleep
 Deaf to my penitential prayer,
Or leave the struggling Bard to weep,
 Alas, and languish in despair?

He is an eagle void of wings
 Aspiring to the mountain's height;
Yet in the vale aloud he sings
 For Pity's aid to give him flight.

Then listen all who never felt
 For fettered genius heretofore—
Let hearts of petrifaction melt
 And bid the gifted Negro soar.

With letter to Horace Greeley, September 11, 1852

The poets ~~feeble~~ petition
G. M. H.

Bewailing mid the ruthless wave
I lift my feeble hand to thee
Let me no longer live a slave
But drop these fetters and be free

Why will regardless fortune sleep
Deaf to my penitential prayer
Or leave the struggling bard to weep
Alas and languish in despair

He is an eagle void of wings
Aspiring to the mountain height
Yet in the vale aloud he sings
For pity's aid to give him flight

Then listen all who never felt
For fettered genius heretofore
Let hearts of petrifaction melt
And ~~bird~~ bid the gifted negro soar

"The Poet's Feeble Petition," 1852, David Lowry Swain Papers, Southern Historical Collection, University of North Carolina, Chapel Hill

FOR THE FAIR MISS M. M. McL[EAN]

An acrostic

May this inspired acrostic prove
A perfect token of my love
Return thy torch allmost expired
Yet find by whom thou art admired

My soul of love would fly to thee
Constrained thy winning form to see

Like pan whose destiny was grief
Exploring nature for relief
And sure when thee my love has found
Nought els[e] in life can heal the wound

When on the constelations
i cast my eyes afar
Then i can tell
My bonny belle
The queen of every star

When i look from the mountain
Or nature's lofty tower
Then i can tell
My bonny belle
The queen of ever[y] flower

When gazing from the window
On blooms both low and tall
Then i can tell
My charming belle
The fairest one of all

Mr. Torence

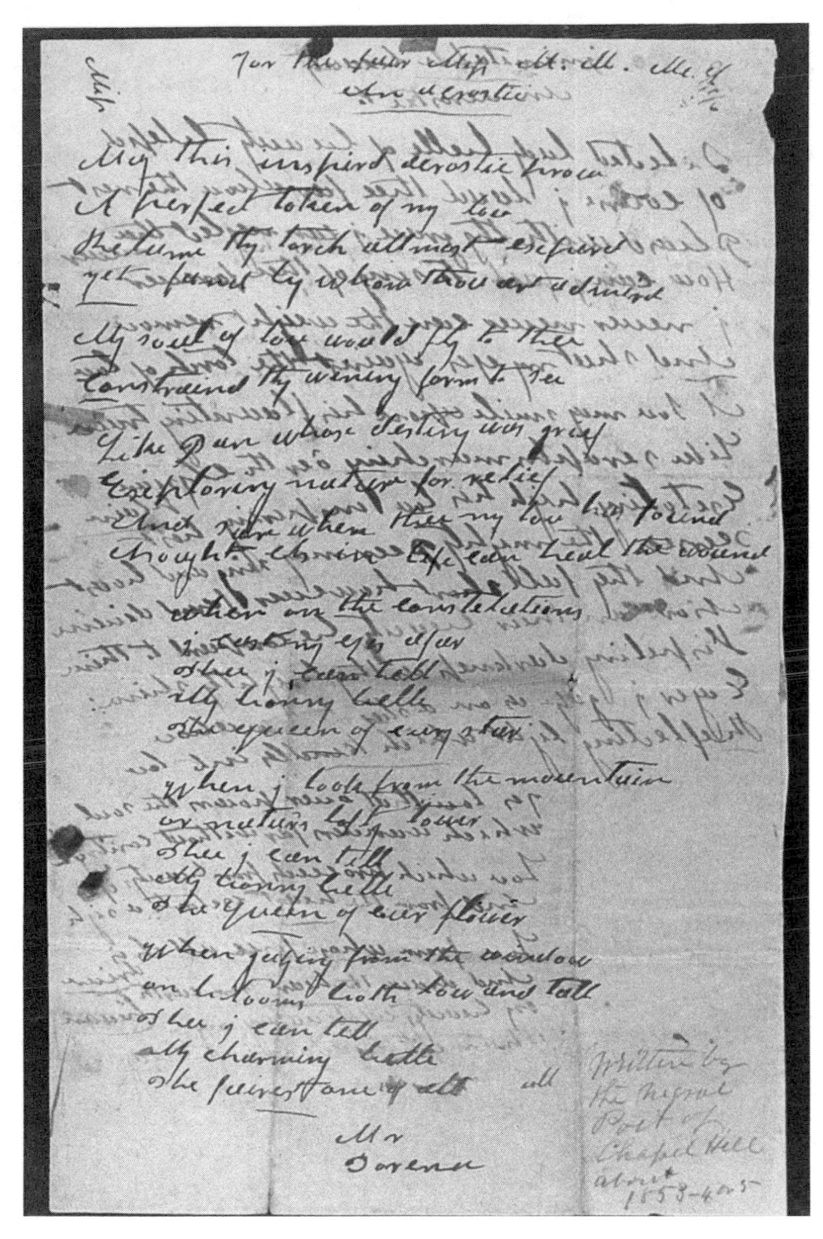

For the fair Miss M. M. McL
An acrostic

May this inspired acrostic prove
A perfect token of my love
Return thy torch almost expired
Yet fanned by whom thou art admired

My soul of love would fly to thee
Constrained thy winning form to see
Like Dan whose destiny was grief
Exploring nature for relief
And now when thee my love hath found
Nought [illegible] life can heal the wound

Either on the constellations
[illegible] my eyes descry
Thee i can tell
My bonny belle
The queen of every star

When i look from the mountain
Or natures loft tower
Thee i can tell
My bonny belle
The queen of ever flower

When peeping from the window
On blooming loth low and tall
Thee i can tell
My charming belle
The fairest one of all

Mr
Horton

Written by the Negro Poet of Chapel Hill about 1853-4 or 5

"*For the fair Miss M. M. McL[ean] An acrostic* [MARY MCLEAN]," *ca.* 1853–55, *Torrance-Banks Family Papers, University of North Carolina at Charlotte Library*

[illegible] following was written by George Haughton the negro poet [illegible]
[illegible] Hill, in the year 1836. W. S. Pettigrew 1

The Emigrant Girl

With pensive thought she leaves her native shore
And ventures dauntless on the unruffl'd lake,
A strange and distant region to explore
But leaves behind no kindred heart to break

The smiles of nature bid the heroess speed
The cloudless heavens and placid air
Why should the waves her lovely flight impede
Or storms obstruct the sail of one so fair

Pensive she sails and yet forbears to speak
Tho oft address'd she scarce a word replys
Her purport is the one she loves to seek
And plough the deep lake with desponding sighs

O'er Erie's dismal wilds behold her borne
The bird of hope still bids her sail along
Till wak'ning numbers with a mournful [illegible]
Arouse expressions from her silent tongue

But soon with much surprise she meets her [illegible]

"The Emigrant Girl," 1836, Pettigrew Family Papers, Southern Historical Collection, University of North Carolina, Chapel Hill

The Emigrant Girl

With jealous marks upon her pallid brow
His pleasing eyes betray his cruel plan
And every look bespeaks a broken vow

Her tears by resignation cease to flow
Still pitious is the case surpass'd by few
Her star-like soul deserts its sphere below
Ascends and bids a treach'rous world adieu

Fair Constance is the partner of her pain
With tears of sympathy the scene to state
A meek eyed Luna mounting from the main
With wings expanded over the gloom of fate

O standing beauty dead her partner crys
Was ever sorrows picture seen before
Reclined she shuts her azure teeming eyes
Her breath is gone alas she lives no more

An acrostic
on the pleasures of beauty [11]

Joy like the morning breaks from one divine
unfailing stream which cannot fail to shine
Long have I strove to magnify her name
imperial floating on the breeze of fame

Attracting beauty must delight afford
Delight of the world and of the bards adored
Her grace of form and heart alluring powers
Express her more than fair, the queen of flowers

Pleasure fond natures stream from beauty sprung
And was the softest strain the muses sung
Converting sorrows into speechless joys
Dispelling gloom which human peace destroys —

Beauty.
But Goddess thou the dimond of the fair
Wilt from thy brow repel affections prayer
And smile to hear the unavailing sigh
With tears dissolving from thy suppliants eye —

But light upon the bride to thee assigned
And leave all els with dismayed behind
Then softly bind affections sacred chain
Never thro life to be broke off again

"An acrostic on the pleasures of beauty [JULIA SHEPARD]," ca. 1835, Pettigrew Family Papers, Southern Historical Collection, University of North Carolina, Chapel Hill

An acrostic by George Horton

Lo: twilight memory's sweet and pleasing beam,
Upon my mind breaks like a morning dream,
Constraining smiles to intermix with tears,
Yet holding fast the scenes of former years,
Gone with the light and shade of joys and fears.
We soon shall close the bright and pleasant scene,
Rejoice with smiles or languish into spleen,
I hail the dawn my constant friends to see,
Glad to rejoice with those who feel for me;
Hope wing me smiling from my long retreat,
The cross was bitter but the crown is sweet.

An acrostic by George Horton the negro bard

Joy may revive in sorrows lonely vale,
And tell the orphan child a cheering tale;
New lustre pour upon her star light mind,
Expelling gloomy childhood far behind;
Explore the litral fields for pleasure true,
Moving from flower to flower entirely new,
Casting thy eye on pleasures known by few,
Immortalise thy-self from love to fame,
Virtue and truth will magnify thy name:
Expand thy mental wing thy worth display,
Rise like a bird and chanting tower away.

Miss Harriet Lane
Raleigh

"An acrostic by George Horton [LUCY G. WRIGHT]," "An acrostic by George Horton the negro bard [JANE E. MCIVER]," n.d., Gillespie and Wright Family Papers, Southern Historical Collection, University of North Carolina, Chapel Hill

THE HOPE

OF

LIBERTY.

CONTAINING

A NUMBER OF POETICAL PIECES.

BY

GEORGE M. HORTON.

RALEIGH:
Printed by J. Gales & Son.
1829.

The title page of The Hope of Liberty. Containing a Number of Poetical Pieces, *North Carolina Collection, University of North Carolina Library, Chapel Hill*

POEMS FROM

The Hope of Liberty

PRAISE OF CREATION

Creation fires my tongue!
   Nature thy anthems raise;
And spread the universal song
   Of thy Creator's praise!

Heaven's chief delight was Man
   Before Creation's birth—
Ordained with joy to lead the van,
   And reign the lord of earth.

When Sin was quite unknown,
   And all the woes it brought,
He hailed the morn without a groan
   Or one corroding thought.

When each revolving wheel
   Assumed its sphere sublime,
Submissive Earth then heard the peal,
   And struck the march of time.

The march in Heaven begun,
   And splendor filled the skies,
When Wisdom bade the morning Sun
   With joy from chaos rise.

The angels heard the tune
   Throughout creation ring;
They seized their golden harps as soon
   And touched on every string.

When time and space were young,
   And music rolled along—
The morning stars together sung,
   And Heaven was drown'd in song.

Ye towering eagles soar,
  And fan Creation's blaze,
And ye terrific lions roar,
  To your Creator's praise.

Responsive thunders roll,
  Loud acclamations sound,
And show your Maker's vast control
  O'er all the worlds around.

Stupendous mountains smoke,
  And lift your summits high,
To him who all your terrors woke,
  Dark'ning the sapphire sky.

Now let my muse descend,
  To view the march below—
Ye subterraneous worlds attend
  And bid your chorus flow.

Ye vast volcanoes yell,
  Whence fiery cliffs are hurled;
And all ye liquid oceans swell
  Beneath the solid world.

Ye cataracts combine,
  Nor let the pæan cease—
The universal concert join,
  Thou dismal precipice.

But halt my feeble tongue,
  My weary muse delays:
But, oh my soul, still float along
  Upon the flood of praise!

ON LIBERTY AND SLAVERY

Alas! and am I born for this,
  To wear this slavish chain?
Deprived of all created bliss,
  Through hardship, toil and pain!

How long have I in bondage lain,
  And languished to be free!
Alas! and must I still complain—
  Deprived of liberty.

Oh, Heaven! and is there no relief
  This side the silent grave—
To soothe the pain—to quell the grief
  And anguish of a slave?

Come Liberty, thou cheerful sound,
  Roll through my ravished ears!
Come, let my brief in joys be drowned,
  And drive away my fears.

Say unto foul oppression, Cease:
  Ye tyrants rage no more,
And let the joyful trump of peace,
  Now bid the vassal soar.

Soar on the pinions of that dove
  Which long has cooed for thee,
And breathed her notes from Afric's grove,
  The sound of Liberty.

Oh, Liberty! thou golden prize,
  So often sought by blood—
We crave thy sacred sun to rise,
  The gift of nature's God!

But Slavery hide her haggard face,
    And barbarism fly:
I scorn to see the sad disgrace
    In which enslaved I lie.

Dear Liberty! upon thy breast,
    I languish to respire;
And like the Swan unto her nest,
    I'd to thy smiles retire.

Oh, blest asylum—heavenly balm!
    Unto thy boughs I flee—
And in thy shades the storm shall calm,
    With songs of Liberty!

Lancaster *Gazette*, April 8, 1828 (as "Liberty and Slavery")
Hope of Liberty (1829)
Emancipator, October 12, 1857

TO ELIZA

Eliza, tell thy lover why
Or what induced thee to deceive me?
Fare thee well—away I fly—
I shun the lass who thus will grieve me.

Eliza, still thou art my song,
Although by force I may forsake thee;
Fare thee well, for I was wrong
To woo thee while another take thee.

Eliza, pause and think awhile—
Sweet lass! I shall forget thee never:
Fare thee well! although I smile,
I grieve to give thee up forever.

Eliza, I shall think of thee—
My heart shall ever twine about thee;
Fare thee well—but think of me,
Compell'd to live and die without thee.
"Fare thee well!—and if forever,
Still forever fare thee well!"

Editor's note: Compare "Fare Thee Well" (stanza 1)
Fare thee well! and if for ever,
Still for ever, fare thee well:
Even though unforgiving, never
'Gainst thee shall my heart rebel.
—Lord Byron (1816)
Compare also Horton's "Farewell to Frances" (1865)

LOVE

Whilst tracing thy visage, I sink in emotion,
   For no other damsel so wond'rous I see;
Thy looks are so pleasing, thy charms so amazing,
   I think of no other, my true-love, but thee.

With heart-burning rapture I gaze on thy beauty,
   And fly like a bird to the boughs of a tree;
Thy looks are so pleasing, thy charms so amazing,
   I fancy no other, my true-love, but thee.

Thus oft in the valley I think, and I wonder
   Why cannot a maid with her lover agree?
Thy looks are so pleasing, thy charms so amazing,
   I pine for no other, my true-love, but thee.

I'd fly from thy frowns with a heart full of sorrow—
   Return, pretty damsel, and smile thou on me;
By every endeavor, I'll try thee forever,
   And languish until I am fancied by thee.

THE SLAVE'S COMPLAINT

Am I sadly cast aside,
On misfortune's rugged tide?
Will the world my pains deride
Forever?

Must I dwell in Slavery's night,
And all pleasure take its flight,
Far beyond my feeble sight,
Forever?

Worst of all, must hope grow dim,
And withhold her cheering beam?
Rather let me sleep and dream
Forever!

Something still my heart surveys,
Groping through this dreary maze;
Is it Hope?—then burn and blaze
Forever!

Leave me not a wretch confined,
Altogether lame and blind—
Unto gross despair consigned,
Forever!

Heaven! in whom can I confide?
Canst thou not for all provide?
Condescend to be my guide
Forever:

And when this transient life shall end,
Oh, may some kind, eternal friend
Bid me from servitude ascend,
Forever!

ON THE TRUTH OF THE SAVIOUR

E'en John the Baptist did not know
   Who Christ the Lord could be,
And bade his own disciples go,
   The strange event to see.

They said, Art thou the one of whom
   'Twas written long before?
Is there another still to come,
   Who will all things restore?

This is enough, without a name—
   Go, tell him what is done;
Behold the feeble, weak and lame,
   With strength rise up and run.

This is enough—the blind now see,
   The dumb Hosannas sing;
Devils far from his presence flee,
   As shades from morning's wing.

See the distress'd, all bathed in tears,
   Prostrate before him fall;
Immanuel speaks, and Lazarus hears—
   The dead obeys his call.

This is enough—the fig-tree dies,
   And withers at his frown;
Nature her God must recognise,
   And drop her flowery crown.

At his command the fish increase,
   And loaves of barley swell—
Ye hungry eat, and hold your peace,
   And find a remnant still.

At his command the water blushed,
  And all was turned to wine,
And in redundance flowed afresh,
  And owned its God divine.

Behold the storms at his rebuke,
  All calm upon the sea—
How can we for another look,
  When none can work as he?

This is enough—it must be God,
  From whom the plagues are driven;
At whose command the mountains nod
  And all the Host of Heaven!

ON SUMMER

Esteville fire begins to burn;
  The auburn fields of harvest rise;
The torrid flames again return,
  And thunders roll along the skies.

Perspiring Cancer lifts his head,
  And roars terrific from on high;
Whose voice the timid creatures dread,
  From which they strive with awe to fly.

The night-hawk ventures from his cell,
  And starts his note in evening air;
He feels the heat his bosom swell,
  Which drives away the gloom of fear.

Thou noisy insect, start thy drum;
  Rise lamp-like bugs to light the train;
And bid sweet Philomela come,
  And sound in front the nightly strain.

The bee begins her ceaseless hum,
  And doth with sweet exertions rise;
And with delight she stores her comb,
  And well her rising stock supplies.

Let sportive children well beware,
  While sprightly frisking o'er the green;
And carefully avoid the snare,
  Which lurks beneath the smiling scene.

The mistress bird assumes her nest,
  And broods in silence on the tree,
Her note to cease, her wings at rest,
  She patient waits her young to see.

The farmer hastens from the heat;
    The weary plough-horse droops his head;
The cattle all at noon retreat,
    And ruminate beneath the shade.

The burdened ox with dauntless rage,
    Flies heedless to the liquid flood,
From which he quaffs, devoid of guage,
    Regardless of his driver's rod.

Pomaceous orchards now expand
    Their laden branches o'er the lea;
And with their bounty fill the land,
    While plenty smiles on every tree.

On fertile borders, near the stream,
    Now gaze with pleasure and delight;
See loaded vines with melons teem—
    'Tis paradise to human sight.

With rapture view the smiling fields,
    Adorn the mountain and the plain,
Each, on the eve of Autumn, yields
    A large supply of golden grain.

ON WINTER

When smiling Summer's charms are past,
  The voice of music dies;
Then Winter pours his chilling blast
  From rough inclement skies.

The pensive dove shuts up her throat,
  The larks forbear to soar,
Or raise one sweet, delightful note,
  Which charm'd the ear before.

The screech-owl peals her shivering tone
  Upon the brink of night;
As some sequestered child unknown,
  Which feared to come in sight.

The cattle all desert the field,
  And eager seek the glades
Of naked trees, which once did yield
  Their sweet and pleasant shades.

The humming insects all are still,
  The beetles rise no more,
The constant tinkling of the bell,
  Along the heath is o'er.

Stern Boreas hurls each piercing gale
  With snow-clad wings along,
Discharging volleys mixed with hail
  Which chill the breeze of song.

Lo, all the Southern windows close,
  Whence spicy breezes roll;
The herbage sinks in sad repose,
  And Winter sweeps the whole.

Thus after youth old age comes on,
   And brings the frost of time,
And e'er our vigor has withdrawn,
   We shed the rose of prime.

Alas! how quick it is the case,
   The scion youth is grown—
How soon it runs its morning race,
   And beauty's sun goes down.

The Autumn of declining years
   Must blanch the father's head,
Encumbered with a load of cares,
   When youthful charms have fled.

HEAVENLY LOVE

Eternal spring of boundless grace!
  It lifts the soul above,
Where God the Son unveils his face,
  And shows that Heaven is love.

Love that revolves through endless years—
  Love that can never pall;
Love which excludes the gloom of fears,
  Love to whom God is all!

Love which can ransom every slave,
  And set the pris'ner free;
Gild the dark horrors of the grave,
  And still the raging sea.

Let but the partial smile of Heaven
  Upon the bosom play,
The mystic sound of sins forgiven,
  Can waft the soul away.

The pilgrim's spirits show this love,
  They often soar on high;
Languish from this dim earth to move,
  And leave the flesh to die.

Sing, oh my soul, rise up and run,
  And leave this clay behind;
Wing thy swift flight beyond the sun,
  Nor dwell in tents confined.

ON THE EVENING AND MORNING

When Evening bids the Sun to rest retire,
Unwearied Ether sets her lamps on fire;
Lit by one torch, each is supplied in turn,
Till all the candles in the concave burn.

The night-hawk now, with his nocturnal tone,
Wakes up, and all the Owls begin to moan,
Or heave from dreary vales their dismal song,
Whilst in the air the meteors play along.

At length the silver queen begins to rise,
And spread her glowing mantle in the skies,
And from the smiling chambers of the east,
Invites the eye to her resplendent feast.

What joy is this unto the rustic swain,
Who from the mount surveys the moon-lit plain;
Who with the spirit of a dauntless *Pan*
Controls his fleecy train and leads the van;

Or pensive, muses on the water's side,
Which purling doth thro' green meanders glide,
With watchful care he broods his heart away
'Till night is swallowed in the flood of day.

The meteors cease to play, that mov'd so fleet,
And spectres from the murky groves retreat,
The prowling wolf withdraws, which howl'd so bold,
And bleating flocks may venture from the fold.

The night-hawk's din deserts the shepherd's ear,
Succeeded by the huntsman's trumpet clear,
O come Diana, start the morning chase
Thou ancient goddess of the hunting race.

Aurora's smiles adorn the mountain's brow,
The peasant hums delighted at his plough,
And lo, the dairy maid salutes her bounteous cow.

Raleigh *Register*, July 18, 1828

ON THE POETIC MUSE

Far, far above this world I soar,
  And almost nature lose,
Aerial regions to explore,
  With this ambitious Muse.

My towering thoughts with pinions rise,
  Upon the gales of song,
Which waft me through the mental skies,
  With music on my tongue.

My Muse is all on mystic fire,
  Which kindles in my breast;
To scenes remote she doth aspire,
  As never yet exprest.

Wrapt in the dust she scorns to lie,
  Call'd by new charms away;
Nor will she e'er refuse to try
  Such wonders to survey.

Such is the quiet bliss of soul,
  When in some calm retreat,
Where pensive thoughts like streamlets roll,
  And render silence sweet;

And when the vain tumultuous crowd
  Shakes comfort from my mind,
My muse ascends above the cloud
  And leaves the noise behind.

With vivid flight she mounts on high
  Above the dusky maze,
And with a perspicacious eye
  Doth far 'bove nature gaze.

Freedom's Journal, August 29, 1828

LINES,

On hearing of the intention of a gentleman
to purchase the Poet's freedom

When on life's ocean first I spread my sail,
I then implored a mild auspicious gale;
And from the slippery strand I took my flight,
And sought the peaceful haven of delight.

Tyrannic storms arose upon my soul,
And dreadful did their mad'ning thunders roll;
The pensive muse was shaken from her sphere,
And hope, it vanished in the clouds of fear.

At length a golden sun broke through the gloom,
And from his smiles arose a sweet perfume—
A calm ensued, and birds began to sing,
And lo! the sacred muse resumed her wing.

With frantic joy she chanted as she flew,
And kiss'd the clement hand that bore her through;
Her envious foes did from her sight retreat,
Or prostrate fall beneath her burning feet.

'Twas like a proselyte, allied to Heaven—
Or rising spirits' boast of sins forgiven,
Whose shout dissolves the adamant away,
Whose melting voice the stubborn rocks obey.

'Twas like the salutation of the dove,
Borne on the zephyr through some lonesome grove,
When Spring returns, and Winter's chill is past,
And vegetation smiles above the blast.

'Twas like the evening of a nuptial pair,
When love pervades the hour of sad despair—
'Twas like fair Helen's sweet return to Troy,
When every Grecian bosom swell'd with joy.

The silent harp which on the osiers hung,
Was then attuned, and manumission sung;
Away by hope the clouds of fear were driven,
And music breathed my gratitude to Heaven.

Hard was the race to reach the distant goal,
The needle oft was shaken from the pole;
In such distress who could forbear to weep?
Toss'd by the headlong billows of the deep!

The tantalizing beams which shone so plain,
Which turned my former pleasures into pain—
Which falsely promised all the joys of fame,
Gave way, and to a more substantial flame.

Some philanthropic souls as from afar,
With pity strove to break the slavish bar;
To whom my floods of gratitude shall roll,
And yield with pleasure to their soft control.

And sure of Providence this work begun—
He shod my feet this rugged race to run;
And in despite of all the swelling tide,
Along the dismal path will prove my guide.

Thus on the dusky verge of deep despair,
Eternal Providence was with me there;
When pleasure seemed to fade on life's gay dawn,
And the last beam of hope was almost gone.

POEMS FROM

The Poetical Works

ON AN OLD DELUDED SUITOR

See sad deluded love in years too late,
With tears desponding o'er the tomb of fate;
While dusky evening's veil excludes the light,
Which in the morning broke upon his sight.
He now regrets his vain, his fruitless plan,
And sadly wonders at the faults of man;
'Tis now from beauty's torch he wheels aside,
And strives to soar above affection's tide;
'Tis now that sorrow feeds the worm of pain
With tears which never can the loss regain;
'Tis now he drinks the wormwood and the gall,
And all the sweets of early pleasures pall;
When from his breast the hope of fortune flies,
The songs of transport languish into sighs.
Fond lovely rose that beamed as she blew,
Of all the charms of youth the most untrue;
She with delusive smiles prevail'd to move
This silly heart into the snares of love.
Then like a flower closed against the bee,
Folds her arms and turns her back on me;
When on my fancy's eye her smile she shed,
The torch by which deluded love was led,
Then like a lark from boyhood's maze I soared,
And thus in song her flattering smiles adored;
My heart was then by fondling love betrayed,
A thousand pleasures bloomed but soon to fade;
From joy to joy my heart exulting flew,
In quest of one though fair, yet far from true.

THE CREDITOR TO HIS PROUD DEBTOR

Ha! tott'ring Johnny strut and boast,
But think of what your feathers cost;
Your crowing days are short at most,
  You bloom but soon to fade.
Surely you could not stand so wide,
If strictly to the bottom tried;
The wind would blow your plume aside,
  If half your debts were paid.
    Then boast and bear the crack,
    With the Sheriff at your back,
    Huzza for dandy Jack,
    My jolly fop, my Joe—

The blue smoke from your segar flies,
Offensive to my nose and eyes,
The most of people would be wise,
  Your presence to evade.
Your pocket jingles loud with cash,
And thus you cut a foppish dash,
But alas! dear boy, you would be trash,
  If your accounts were paid.
    Then boast and bear the crack, &c.

My duck bill boots would look as bright,
Had you in justice served me right,
Like you, I then could step as light,
  Before a flaunting maid.
As nicely could I clear my throat,
And to my tights, my eyes devote,
But I'd leave you bare without that coat,
  For which you have not paid.
    Then boast and bear the crack, &c.

I'd toss myself with a scornful air,
And to a poor man pay no care,
I could rock cross-legged on my chair,
    Within the cloister shade.
I'd gird my neck with a light cravat,
And creaning wear my bell-crown hat;
But away my down would fly at that,
    If once my debts were paid.
        Then boast and bear the crack,
        With a Sheriff at your back,
        Huzza for dandy Jack,
        My jolly fop, my Joe—

THE RETREAT FROM MOSCOW

Sad Moscow, thy fate do I see,
  Fire, fire, in the city all cry;
Like quails from the eagle all flee,
  Escape in a moment or die.

It looks like the battle of Troy,
  The storm rises higher and higher;
The scene of destruction all hearts must annoy,
  The whirlwinds, the smoke and the fire.

The dread conflagration rolls forth,
  Augmenting the rage of the wind,
Which blows it from south unto north,
  And leaves but the embers behind.

It looks like Gomorrah the flame,
  Is moving still higher and higher;
Aloud from all quarters the people proclaim,
  The whirlwind, the smoke and the fire.

A dead fumigation now swells,
  A blue circle darkens the air,
With tones as the pealing of bells,
  Farewell to the brave and the fair.

O, Moscow, thou city of grace,
  Consigned to a dread burning pyre,
From morning to ev'ning, with sorrow I trace,
  The wild winds, the smoke and the fire.

The dogs in the kennel all howl,
  The wether takes flight with the ox;
Appall'd on the wing is the fowl,
  The pigeon deserting her box.

With a heart full of pain in the night,
 'Mid hillocks and bogs I retire;
Through lone deadly valleys I steer by its light,
 The wild storm, the smoke and the fire.

Though far the crash breaks on my ear,
 The stars glimmer dull in the sky;
The shrieks of the women I hear,
 The fall of the kingdom is nigh.

O, Heaven, when earth is no more,
 And all things in nature expire;
May I thus, with safety keep distant before,
 The whirlwind, the smoke and the fire.

It well bespeaks a man beheaded, quite
Divested of the laurel robe of life,
When every member struggles for its base;
The head, the power of order, now recedes,
Unheeded efforts rise on every side,
With dull emotion rolling through the brain
Of apprehending slaves. The flocks and herds
In sad confusion now run to and fro,
And seem to ask, distressed, the reason why
That they are thus prostrated. Howl, ye dogs!
Ye cattle, low! Ye sheep, astonish'd, bleat!
Ye bristling swine, trudge squealing through the glades,
Void of an owner to impart your food.
Sad horses, lift your head and neigh aloud,
And caper, frantic, from the dismal scene;
Mow the last food upon your grass clad lea,
And leave a solitary home behind,
In hopeless widowhood, no longer gay.
The trav'ling sun of gain his journey ends
In unavailing pain; he sets with tears—
A King, sequestered, sinking from his throne,
Succeeded by a train of busy friends,
Like stars which rise with smiles to mark the flight
Of awful Phoebus to another world.
Stars after stars in fleet succession rise,
Into the wide empire of fortune clear,
Regardless of the donor of their lamps,
Like heirs forgetful of parental care,
Without a grateful smile or filial tear,
Redound in reverence to expiring age.
But soon parental benediction flies
Like vivid meteors in a moment gone,
As though they ne'er had been; but O, the state,
The dark suspense in which poor vassals stand;
Each mind upon the spire of chance hangs, fluctuant,

The day of separation is at hand.
Imagination lifts her gloomy curtain
Like ev'ning's mantle at the flight of day,
Through which the trembling pinnacle we spy,
On which we soon must stand with hopeful smiles,
Or apprehending frowns, to tumble on
The right or left forever.

IMPLORING TO BE RESIGNED AT DEATH

Let me die and not tremble at death,
  But smile at the close of my day,
And then at the flight of my breath,
  Like a bird of the morning in may,
    Go chanting away.

Let me die without fear of the dead,
  No horrors my soul shall dismay,
And with faith's pillow under my head,
  With defiance to mortal decay,
    Go chanting away.

Let me die like a son of the brave,
  And martial distinction display;
Nor shrink from a thought of the grave,
  No, but with a smile from the clay,
    Go chanting away.

Let me die glad, regardless of pain,
  No pang to this world [to] betray,
And the spirit cut loose from its chains,
  So loath in the flesh to delay
    Go chanting away.

Let me die, and my worst foe forgive,
  When death veils the last vital ray;
Since I have but a moment to live,
  Let me, when the last debt I pay,
    Go chanting away.

THE GRADUATE LEAVING COLLEGE

What summons do I hear?
    The morning peal, departure's knell;
My eyes let fall a friendly tear,
    And bid this place farewell.

Attending servants come,
    The carriage wheels like thunders roar,
To bear the pensive seniors home,
    Here to be seen no more.

Pass one more transient night,
    The morning sweeps the College clean;
The graduate takes his last long flight,
    No more in College seen.

The bee, in which courts the flower,
    Must with some pain itself employ,
And then fly, at the day's last hour,
    Home to its hive with joy.

EARLY AFFECTION

I lov'd thee from the earliest dawn,
When first I saw thy beauty's ray,
And will, until life's eve comes on,
And beauty's blossom fades away;
And when all things go well with thee,
With smiles and tears remember me.

I'll love thee when thy morn is past,
And wheedling gallantry is o'er,
When youth is lost in ages blast,
And beauty can ascend no more,
And when life's journey ends with thee
O, then look back and think of me.

I'll love thee with a smile or frown,
'Mid sorrow's gloom or pleasure's light,
And when the chain of life runs down,
Pursue thy last eternal flight,
When thou hast spread thy wing to flee,
Still, still, a moment wait for me.

I'll love thee for those sparkling eyes,
To which my fondness was betray'd,
Bearing the tincture of the skies,
To glow when other beauties fade,
And when they sink too low to see,
Reflect an azure beam on me.

REFLECTIONS FROM THE FLASH OF A METEOR

Psalm XC. 12

So teach me to regard my day,
How small a point my life appears;
One gleam to death the whole betrays,
A momentary flash of years.

One moment smiles, the scene is past,
Life's gaudy bloom at once we shed;
And sink beneath affliction's blast,
Or drop as soon among the dead.

Short is the chain wound up at morn,
Which oft runs down and stops at noon;
Thus in a moment man is born,
And lo! the creature dies as soon.

Life's little torch, how soon forgot,
Dim burning on its dreary shore;
Just like that star which downwards shot,
It glimmers and is seen no more.

Teach me to draw this transient breath,
With conscious awe my end to prove;
Early to make my peace with death,
As thus in haste from time we move.

O Heaven, through this murky vale,
Direct me with a burning pen;
Thus shall I, on a tuneful gale,
Fleet on my three score years and ten.

Editor's note: Psalm 90:12 reads: "So teach us to number our days, that we may apply our hearts unto wisdom."

THE FATE OF AN INNOCENT DOG

When Tiger left his native yard,
He did not many ills regard,
    A fleet and harmless cur;
Indeed he was a trusty dog,
And did not through the pasture prog,
The grazing flock to stir, poor dog.
    The grazing flocks to stir.

He through a field by chance was led
In quest of game, not far ahead,
    And made one active leap,
When all at once, alarmed, he spied
A creature weltering on its side,
A deadly wounded sheep, alas!
    A deadly wounded sheep.

He there was filled with sudden fear,
Apprised of lurking danger near,
    And there he left his trail;
Indeed, he was afraid to yelp,
Nor could he grant the creature help,
But wheeled and dropped his tail, poor dog,
    But wheeled and dropped his tail.

It was his pastime, pride and fun,
At morn the nimble hare to run,
    When frost was on the grass;
Returning home, who should he meet,
The wether's owner coming fleet,
Who scorned to let him pass, alas!
    Who scorned to let him pass.

Tiger could but his bristles raise,
A surly complement he pays,
    Insulted shows his wrath,
Returns a just defensive growl,

And does not turn aside to prowl,
But onward keeps the path, poor dog!
  But onward keeps the path.

The raging owner found the brute,
But could afford no recruit,
  Nor raise it up to stand;
'Twas mangled by some other dogs,
A set of detrimental rogues,
Raised up at no command, alas!
  Raised up at no command.

Sagacious tiger left his bogs,
But bore the blame of other dogs,
  With powder, fire and ball;
They killed the poor unlawful game,
And then came back and eat the same,
But tiger paid for all, poor dog,
  But tiger paid for all.

Let every harmless dog beware,
Lest he be taken in the snare;
  And scorn such fields to roam,
A creature may be fraught with grace,
And suffer for the vile and base,
By straggling off from home, alas!
  By straggling off from home.

The blood of creatures oft is spilt,
Who die without a shade of guilt—
  Look out or cease to roam—
Whilst up and down, the world he plays,
For pleasure, man, in danger strays,
Without a friend from home, alas!
  Without a friend from home.

ON THE PLEASURES OF COLLEGE LIFE

. . . .

Such are the liberal charms of college life,
Where pleasure flows without a breeze of strife;
And such would be my pain if cast away,
Without the bloom of study to display.

. . . .

Where brooding Milton's theme purls sweet along
With Pope upon the gales of epic song;
Where you may trace a bland Demosthenes,
Whose oratoric pen ne'er fails to please.
And Plato, with immortal Cicero,
And with the eloquence of Horace glow;

. . . .

Now let us take a retrospective view,
And whilst we pause, observe a branch or two.
Geography and Botany unfold
Their famous charms like precious seeds of gold;
Zoology doth all her groups descry,
And with Astronomy we soar on high;
But pen and ink and paper all will fail,
To write one third of this capacious tale.

. . . .

Zoology, with her delightful strain,
Doth well the different animals explain;
From multipedes to emmets in the dust,
And all the groveling reptiles of disgust;
She well descries the filthy beetle blind,
With insects high and low of every kind;
She with her microscope surveys the mite,
Which ne'er could be beheld by naked sight;
Thence she descends into the boundless deep,
Where dolphins play and monsters slowly creep;
Explores the foaming main from shore to shore,
And hears with awe the d[a]shing sea bull roar;
Traces enormous whales exploding high
Their floods of briny water to the sky;

Describes the quadrupeds of every shape,
The bear, the camel, elephant and ape,
And artful monkey, which but lacks to talk,
And like the human kind uprightly walk.

. . . .

But nature never yet was half explored,
Though by philosopher and bard adored;
Astronomer and naturalist expire,
And languish that they could ascend no higher;
Expositors of words in every tongue,
Writers of prose and scribblers of song,
Would fail with all their mathematic powers,
And vainly study out their fleeting hours.

. . . .

Volume Divine! O thou the sacred dew,
Thy fadeless fields see elders passing through;
thy constant basis must support the whole,
The cabinet and alcove of the soul;
It matters not through what we may have pass'd,
To thee for sure support we fly at last;
Encyclopedias we may wander o'er,
And study every scientific lore;
Ancient and modern authors we may read,
The soul must starve or on thy pastures feed.

. . . .

Theology, thou sweetest science yet,
Beneath whose boughs the silent classics sit,
And thus imbibe the sacred rays divine,
Which make the mitred faculty to shine;

. . . .

Such is the useful graduate indeed,
Not merely at the bar in law to plead,
Nor a physician best to heal the flesh;
On such a senior let archangels smile,
And all the students imitate his style,

Who bears with joy the mission all divine,
The beams of sanctitude, A Paul benign,
Whose sacred call is to evangelize,
A gospel prince, a legate of the skies,
Whose bright diploma is a deed from heaven
The palm of love, the wreath of sins forgiven.

CONNUBIAL FELICITY

The fairest soonest fade,
Young brides in flowers array'd,
  Will soon grow old,
  And prove a scold,
Tho' their forms decay'd.

But would you live with her at ease,
  Fly from the elf and leave her;
The only means a dame to please
  Is by your flight to grieve her.

The sweetest soonest pall,
The tallest soonest fall;
  The tender bloom,
  Of sweet perfume,
Will pine the first of all.

Little regard the ills of life,
  Her frowns are but to flatter;
So when your flight has grieved your wife,
  Come back and discord scatter.

The gaudy charms of May,
Are quickly past away;
  The honey moon
  Will change as soon,
And love to ills betray.

The fairest fruit upon the tree
  Is ever soonest rotten;
Know in as much the nuptial glee
  Must pass and be forgotten.

THE TIPPLER TO HIS BOTTLE

What hast thou ever done for me?
  Defeated every good endeavor;
I never can through life agree
To place my confidence in thee,
    Not ever! no, never!

Often have I thy stream admired,
  Thou nothing hast availed me ever;
Vain have I thought myself inspired;
Say have I else but pain acquired?
    Not ever! no, never!

No earthly good, no stream of health,
  Flows from thy fount thou cheerful giver,
From thee affluence sinks to stealth,
From thee I pluck no bloom of health,
    Whatever! no, never!

Thou canst impart a noble mind,
  Power from my tongue flows like a river,
The gas flows dead I'm left behind,
To all that's evil down confined,
    To flourish more, never!

With thee I must through life complain,
  Thy powers at large will union sever;
Disgorge no more thy killing bane,
The bird, hope, flies from thee in pain,
    To return more, never!

MEDITATION ON A COLD, DARK AND RAINY NIGHT

Sweet on the house top falls the gentle shower,
When jet black darkness crowns the silent hour,
When shrill the owlet pours her hollow tone,
Like some lost child sequester'd and alone,
When Will's bewildering wisp begins to flare,
And Philomela breathes her dulcet air,
'Tis sweet to listen to her nightly tune,
Deprived of starlight or the smiling moon.

When deadly winds sweep round the rural shed,
And tell of strangers lost without a bed,
Fond sympathy invokes her dol'rous lay,
And pleasure steals in sorrow's gloom away,
Till fost'ring Somnus bids my eyes to close,
And smiling visions open to repose;
Still on my soothing couch I lie at ease,
Still round my chamber flows the whistling breeze.

Still in the chain of life I lie confined,
To all the threat'ning ills of life resigned;
Regardless of the wandering elfs of night,
While phantoms break on my immortal sight;
The trump of morning bids my slumber end,
While from a flood of light I straight ascend,
When on a busy world I cast my eyes,
And think of nightly slumbers with surprise.

THE FEARFUL TRAVELLER IN THE HAUNTED CASTLE

Oft do I hear those windows ope
  And shut with dread surprise,
And spirits murmur as they grope,
  But break not on the eyes.

Still fancy spies the winding sheet,
  The phantom and the shroud,
And bids the pulse of horror beat
  Throughout my ears aloud.

Some unknown finger thumps the door,
  From one of falt'ring voice,
Till some one seems to walk the floor
  With an alarming noise.

The drum of horror holds her sound,
  Which will not let me sleep,
When ghastly breezes float around,
  And hidden goblins creep.

Methinks I hear some constant groan,
  The din of all the dead,
While trembling thus I lie alone,
  Upon this restless bed.

At length the blaze of morning broke
  On my impatient view,
And truth or fancy told the joke,
  And bade the night adieu.

'Twas but the noise of prowling rats,
  Which ran with all their speed,
Pursued in haste by hungry cats,
  Which on the vermin feed.

The cat growl'd as she held her prey,
   Which shrieked with all its might,
And drove the balm of sleep away
   Throughout the live-long night.

Those creatures crumbling off the cheese
   Which on the table lay,
Some cats too quick the rogues to seize,
   With rumbling lost their prey.

Thus man is often, his own self,
   Who makes the night his ghost,
And shrinks with horror from himself,
   Which is to fear the most.

Editor's note: Compare the last stanza with Emily Dickinson, "One need not be a Chamber—to be Haunted—" (ca. 1863)

Far safer, of a Midnight Meeting
External Ghost
Than its interior Confronting—
That Cooler Host.

. . . .

Ourself behind ourself, concealed—
Should startle most—
Assassin hid in our Apartment
Be Horror's least.

TROUBLED WITH THE ITCH, AND RUBBING WITH SULPHUR

'Tis bitter, yet 'tis sweet;
    Scratching effects but transient ease;
Pleasure and pain together meet
    And vanish as they please.

My nails, the only balm,
    To every bump are oft applied,
And thus the rage will sweetly calm
    Which aggravates my hide.

It soon returns again:
    A frown succeeds to every smile;
Grinning I scratch and curse the pain
    But grieve to be so vile.

In fine, I know not which
    Can play the most deceitful game:
The devil, sulphur, or the itch.
    The three are but the same.

The devil sows the itch,
    And sulphur has a loathsome smell,
And with my clothes as black as pitch,
    I stink where'er I dwell.

Excoriated deep,
    By friction played on every part,
It oft deprives me of my sleep
    And plagues me to my heart.

Throughout our rambles much we find,
  The bee trees burst with honey;
Wild birds we tame of ev'ry kind,
At once they seem to be resigned;
I know but one that lags behind—
  There's nothing lags but money.

The woods afford us much supply,
  The opossum, coon and coney;
They are all tame and venture nigh,
Regardless of the public eye;
I know but one among them shy,
  There's nothing shy but money.

And she lies in the bankrupt shade,
  The cunning fox is funny;
When thus the public debts are paid,
Deceitful cash is not afraid,
Where funds are hid for private trade,
  There's nothing paid but money.

Thou let us roam the woods along,
  And drive the coon and coney;
Our lead is good, our powder strong,
To shoot the pigeons as they throng,
But sing no more the idle song,
  Nor prowl the chase for money.

MAN, A TORCH

Blown up with painful care and hard to light,
A glimmering torch blown in a moment out,
Suspended by a web, an angler's bait,
Floating at stake along the stream of chance,
Snatch'd from its hook by the fish of poverty,
A silent cavern is his last abode;
The king's repository veil'd with gloom,
The umbrage of a thousand oziers bowed,
The couch of hallowed bones, the grave's asylum,
The brave's retreat and end of ev'ry care.

POEMS FROM

Naked Genius

NAKED GENIUS:

BY

GEORGE MOSES HORTON,

THE COLORED BARD OF NORTH CAROLINA.

AUTHOR OF "THE BLACK POET,"

A WORK BEING NOW COMPILED AND REVISED BY CAPTAIN WILL. H. S. BANKS, 9TH MICHIGAN CAVALRY VOLUNTEERS, AND WHICH WILL BE READY FOR PUBLICATION ABOUT THE 1ST OF OCTOBER, 1865. THIS WORK WILL CONTAIN A CONCISE HISTORY OF THE LIFE OF THE AUTHOR, WRITTEN BY THE COMPILER, AND WILL BE OFFERED TO THE PUBLIC AS ONE OF THE MANY PROOFS THAT GOD, IN HIS INFINITE WISDOM AND MERCY, CREATED THE BLACK MAN FOR A HIGHER AND NOBLER PURPOSE THAN TO TOIL HIS LIFE AWAY UNDER THE GALLING YOKE OF SLAVERY.

REVISED AND COMPILED BY

WILL. H. S. BANKS,

CAPT. 9TH MICH. CAV.

WM. B. SMITH & CO.:

SOUTHERN FIELD AND FIRESIDE BOOK PUBLISHING HOUSE,

RALEIGH, N. C.

1865.

The title page of Naked Genius, *North Carolina Collection, University of North Carolina Library, Chapel Hill*

GEORGE MOSES HORTON, MYSELF

I feel myself in need
Of the inspiring strains of ancient lore,
My heart to lift, my empty mind to feed,
And all the world explore.

I know that I am old
And never can recover what is past,
But for the future may some light unfold
And soar from ages blast.

I feel resolved to try,
My wish to prove, my calling to pursue,
Or mount up from the earth into the sky,
To show what Heaven can do.

My genius from a boy,
Has fluttered like a bird within my heart;
But could not thus confined her powers employ,
Impatient to depart.

She, like a restless bird,
Would spread her wing, her power to be unfurl'd,
And let her songs be loudly heard,
And dart from world to world.

GEN. GRANT—THE HERO OF THE WAR

Brave Grant, thou hero of the war,
Thou art the emblem of the morning star,
Transpiring from the East to banish fear,
Revolving o'er a servile Hemisphere,
At large thou hast sustained the chief command
And at whose order all must rise and stand,
To hold position in the field is thine,
To sink in darkness or to rise and shine.

Thou art the leader of the Fed'ral band,
To send them at thy pleasure through the land,
Whose martial soldiers never did recoil
Nor fail in any place to take the spoil,
Thus organized was all the army firm,
And led unwavering to their lawful term,
Never repulsed or made to shrink with fear,
Advancing in their cause so truly dear.

The love of Union burned in every heart,
Which led them true and faithful from the start,
Whether upon water or on land,
They all obeyed their marshal's strict command,
By him the regiments were all surveyed,
His trumpet voice was by the whole obeyed,
His order right was every line to form,
And all be well prepared to front the storm.

Ye Southern gentlemen must grant him praise,
Nor on the flag of Union fail to gaze;
Ye ladies of the South forego the prize,
Our chief commander here to recognize,
From him the stream of general orders flow,
And every chief on him some praise bestow,
The well-known victor of the mighty cause
Demands from every voice a loud applause.

What more has great Napoleon ever done,
Though many battles in his course he won?
What more has Alexander e'er achieved,
Who left depopulated cities grieved?
To him we dedicate the whole in song,
The verses from our pen to him belong,
To him the Union banners are unfurled,
The star of peace the standard of the world.

THE SOUTHERN REFUGEE

What sudden ill the world await,
From my dear residence I roam;
I must deplore the bitter fate,
To straggle from my native home.

The verdant willow droops her head,
And seems to bid a fare thee well;
The flowers with tears their fragrance shed,
Alas! their parting tale to tell.

'Tis like the loss of Paradise,
Or Eden's garden left in gloom,
Where grief affords us no device;
Such is thy lot, my native home.

I never, never shall forget
My sad departure far away,
Until the sun of life is set,
And leaves behind no beam of day.

How can I from my seat remove
And leave my ever devoted home,
And the dear garden which I love,
The beauty of my native home?

Alas! sequestered, set aside,
It is a mournful tale to tell;
'Tis like a lone deserted bride
That bade her bridegroom fare thee well.

I trust I soon shall dry the tear
And leave forever hence to roam,
Far from a residence so dear,
The place of beauty—my native home.

JEFFERSON IN A TIGHT PLACE

The Fox Is Caught

The blood hounds, long upon the trail,
Have rambled faithful, hill and dale;
But mind, such creatures never fail,
    To run the rebel down.
His fears forbid him long to stop,
Altho' he gains the mountain top,
He soon is made his tail to drop,
    And fleets to leave the hounds.

Alas! he speeds from place to place,
Such is the fox upon the chase;
To him the mud is no disgrace,
    No lair his cause defends.
He leaves a law and seeks a dell,
And where to fly 'tis hard to tell;
He fears before to meet with hell;
    Behind he has no friends.

But who can pity such a fox,
Though buried among the rocks?
He's a nuisance among the flocks,
    And sucks the blood of geese.
He takes advantage of the sheep,
His nature is at night to creep,
And rob the flocks while the herdsmen sleep,
    When dogs can have no peace.

But he is now brought to a bay,
However fast he run away,
He knows he has not long to stay,
    And assumes a raccoon's dress.
Found in a hole, he veils his face,
And fain would take a lady's place,
But fails, for he has run his race,
    And falls into distress.

The fox is captured in his den,
The martial troops of Michigan
May hence be known the fleetest men,
  For Davis is their prey.
Great Babylon has fallen down,
A King is left without a crown,
Stripped of honors and renown,
  The evening ends the day.

Editor's note: Jefferson Davis was president of the Confederacy.

LINCOLN IS DEAD

He is gone, the strong base of the nation,
  The dove to his covet has fled;
Ye heroes lament his privation,
  For Lincoln is dead.

He is gone down, the sun of the Union,
  Like Phoebus, that sets in the west;
The planet of peace and communion,
  Forever has gone to his rest.

He is gone down from a world of commotion,
  No equal succeeds in his stead;
His wonders extend with the ocean,
  Whose waves murmur, Lincoln is dead.

He is gone and can ne'er be forgotten,
  Whose great deeds eternal shall bloom;
When gold, pearls and diamonds are rotten,
  His deeds will break forth from the tomb.

He is gone out of glory to glory,
  A smile with the tear may be shed,
O, then let us tell the sweet story,
  Triumphantly, Lincoln is dead.

THE CHEERLESS CONDITION OF BACHELORSHIP

When Adam dwelt in Eden's shades alone,
He breathed to heaven a sad and piteous tone;
For nothing pleasing yet the world displayed,
Though he the blooming garden well surveyed.

Throughout the place no pleasing sound he heard,
No lovely scene unto his eye appeared;
Lone man was then a hermit, quite retired,
Whose flowery cot no cupid had inspired.

His maker said, he is not well alone,
Hence from his side I will extract a bone;
By an etheral opiate, sound and deep,
Man on his side was prostrate laid asleep.

Fresh to his view the smiling vision rose,
The queen of pleasure in his calm repose;
He woke in wonder from his pleasing dream,
To sing and tell it to the limpid stream.

When lo! he saw the bridal vision rise,
On whom he gazed with rapture and surprise;
Her charm was heaven, her visage glowed with love,
Whose smiles reflected grace thro' all the grove;
Thus did her glory crown the martial [marital] bower,
The rosy maid and queen of every flower.

The birds of Hymen struck the wondrous song,
And fragrant breezes flowed with peace along;
Myriads of beasts flocked round their festive place,
Which pranced and bellowed round the scene of grace.

Then Philomena tuned her lyric tongue,
And rung all night the hymenial song;
Such is the happy change of single life,
And such the pain of man without a wife;
No smiling dame his pleasures to divide,
A perfect stranger to a loving bride.

Nay, man alone is but a frantic elf,
A troubled sea, a burden to himself;
Without the knowledge of connubial bliss,
And what is life in such a state as this?

Melancholy wile, the stormy night,
The fluctuating vessel never right;
A clouded sky, a dull and sunless day,
A week which passes void of rest away.

Man strikes the road of fortune in his youth,
Which quickly ends, but seldom ends in truth;
Upon her plume he first directs his eyes,
Which lightly plays, but far before him flies;
Which, when he gains is withered by the blast,
And all his fond design is lost at last.

Mistaken man, the dearest gem is love,
The diamond which forbids the mind to rove;
The pride of nature, or the soothing wife,
The soul of pleasure, and the palm of life.

THE SLAVE

What right divine has mortal man received,
To domineer with uncontroll'd command?
What philosophic wight has thus believed
That Heaven entailed on him the weaker band?

If Africa was fraught with weaker light,
Whilst to the tribes of Europe more was given,
Does this impart to them a lawful right
To counterfeit the golden rule of Heaven?

Did sovereign justice give to robbery birth,
And bid the fools to theft their rights betray,
To spread the seeds of slavery o'er the earth,
That you should hold them as your lawful prey?

Why did Almighty God the land divide
And bid each nation to maintain her own,
Rolling between the deep, the wind and tide,
With all their rage to make his order known?

The sad phylactory bound on rebel Cain,
For killing Abel is in blood reveal'd,
For which the soldier falls among the slain,
A victim on the sanguinary field.

Thus, in the cause of vile and sordid gain,
To gratify their lust is all the plea;
Like Cain you've your consanguine brother slain,
And robbed him of his birthright—Liberty.

Why do ye not the Ishmealites enslave,
Or artful red man in his rude attire,
As well as with the Black man, split the wave,
And to his progeny with rage aspire?

Because the brood-sow's left side pigs were black,
  Whose sable tincture was by nature struck,
Are you by justice bound to pull them back
  And leave the sandy colored pigs to suck?

Or can you deem that God does not intend
  His kingdom through creation to display,
The sacred right of nature to defend,
  And show to mortals who shall bear the sway?

Then suffer Heaven to vindicate the cause,
  The wrong abolish and the right restore;
To make a sacrifice of cruel laws,
  And slavish murmurs will be heard no more.

NEW FASHIONS

There was a time when death was terror,
Something harsh in every ear,
The tear left on the cheek a furrow,
And every breath was drawn with fear;
Now the pall soon dies away,
Bury the dead and all be gay.

. . . .

There was a time that rare was danger,
Dirks and pistols slept profound;
Thus sustain the harmless stranger,
And the peasant was renowned;
Now all cry take care cut throat,
Long moustaches, caps and boots.

There was a time when rules were riches,
Wives and husbands knew their own;
Women seldom wore the breeches,
Left their husbands' ploughs alone;
Now tobacco rules have crossed,
And no one knows who chaws the most.

There was a time when peace was plenty,
All the world could harmonize;
Few complained, not one in twenty,
Of good peas and pumpkin pies;
Soda shortens now the meal,
Else you'll hear a dreadful peal.

. . . .

There was a time when ladies swore not,
Teasing their husbands for a dram;
Draughts of gin their bosoms bore not,
Effusing from their lips a damn;
Now they swear, they drink and boast,
And the fairest drink the most.

. . . .

ONE GENERATION PASSETH AWAY AND ANOTHER COMETH

From world to world, unknown we speed,
And leave the globe where first we try;
While others to our place succeed,
And in a moment die.

Alas, we know not whence we came,
To tarry but a transient day;
Break into time to gather fame,
And pass at once away.

At once we rise and fix our snares,
To catch the flitting birds of gain;
'Till burdened with a thousand cares,
And life turns into pain.

Vain bird, a while think what am I,
Here entering 'mid a hawk-like throng;
Quickly hatched out, as quick to fly,
And dare not tarry long.

Where is the mighty and the stout,
Who lived this fading world to crave?
Left and forever gone without
A stone to show their grave.

Psalm 37, v. 36

Editor's note: Psalm 37:36 reads:
"Yet he passed away, and, lo, he was not:
yea, I sought him, but he could not be found."

SONG OF LIBERTY AND PARENTAL ADVICE

Come help me sing the morning song,
   While woods are sweetly blooming,
And bears the joyful strain along,
   That happier days are coming.

. . . . . .

Let other people's goods alone,
   But raise yourself a plenty;
To delve and cultivate your own,
   And beg not one in twenty.

How dare you touch another's spoil,
   When you have strength to labor?
Oh, then be glad to dig and toil,
   And let alone your neighbor.

. . . .

Your wife may well be busy too,
   Averting all starvation;
Keep clean herself, her house and you,
   And thus support her station.

. . . .

Close labor works you up to wealth,
   It makes your wife to love you;
If sick it oft restores to health,
   Tho' idlers may reprove you.

Thus did a man his son advise,
   Let not your friends deceive you,
If in the world you wish to rise,
   Take care of what I give you.

. . . .

Another lesson you would give,
   Hold in your feet from rambling;
By straggling you can never live,
   By sporting nor by gambling.

Take not the bottle for your friend,
For this will sure deceive you,
And this you may in truth depend,
Both health and wealth will leave you.

It robs you of your rest at night,
Take money, fame and pleasure,
Which never can the loss requite,
But drains the fount of pleasure.

DEATH OF AN OLD CARRIAGE HORSE

I was a harness horse,
Constrained to travel weak or strong,
With orders from oppressing force,
Push along, push along.

I had no space of rest,
And took at forks the roughest prong,
Still by the cruel driver pressed,
Push along, push along.

Vain strove the idle bird,
To charm me with her artless song,
But pleasure lingered from the word,
Push along, push along.

The order of the day
Was push, the peal of every tongue,
The only word was all the way,
Push along, push along.

Thus to my journey's end,
Had I to travel right or wrong,
'Till death my sweet and favored friend,
Bade me from life to push along.

THE CLOSE OF LIFE

To the scene of life now closes
  Time, farewell to thee;
Oh! that I could die like Moses,
  Drop and strangely flee;
I'm gone, amen—I'm gone forever,
  My eternal debt to pay;
To return again more never,
  Torn from earth away.

Flesh and spirit clept asunder,
  With the flight of breath;
Halt my soul, look down and wonder,
  After gloom of death;
But let no sobbing tones attend it,
  Hide! oh hide! the lifeless frame;
Sobs and tears can never mend it,
  All must die the same.

Man is born not long to tarry,
  A bloom of swift decay;
Death like lightning flies to carry
  Souls from time away.
His worthless jaw is but a bubble,
  Mortal, what is fortune's crown.
Groping thro' a maze of trouble,
  What is vain renown.

Life is but a cloud of sorrow,
  Oh! but soon to close;
I'm here today, but gone to-morrow,
  To my long repose.
See, see, how fast in fate's dark ocean,
  Mortals sink beneath the wave;
From a stage of proud devotion,
  Onward to the grave.

Life's dull blush, no spring retrieves it,
  Left without a bloom;
Which, when transient summer leaves it,
  Blossoms for the tomb.
Then, oh my soul, forbear to languish,
  Drop thy mantle on the shore;
Sing, oh death, where is thy anguish,
  Lost and felt no more.

A SLAVE'S REFLECTIONS THE EVE BEFORE HIS SALE

O, comrades! to-morrow we try,
 The fate of an exit unknowing—
Tears trickled from every eye—
 'Tis going, 'tis going, 'tis going!

Who shall the dark problem then solve,
 An evening of gladness or sorrow,
Thick clouds of emotion evolve,
 The sun which awaits us to-morrow,
 O! to-morrow! to-morrow!
Thick clouds of emotion evolve,
 The sun which awaits us to-morrow.

Soon either with smiles or with tears,
 Will the end of our course be completed.
The progress of long fleeting years,
 Triumphant or sadly regretted.

In whom shall the vassal confide,
 On a passage so treacherous and narrow,
What tongue shall the question decide,
 The end which awaits us to-morrow?
 O! to-morrow, to-morrow!
What tongue shall the question decide,
 The end which awaits us to-morrow?

The sun seems with doubt to look down,
 As he rides on his chariot of glory,
A king with a torch and a crown,
 But fears to exhibit his story.

What pen the condition makes known,
O! prophet thy light would I borrow,
To steer through the desert alone,
And gaze on the fate of to-morrow;
O! to-morrow, to-morrow!
To steer through the desert alone,
And gaze on the fate of to-morrow.

FAREWELL TO FRANCES

Farewell! If ne'er I see thee more,
   Though distant calls my flight impel,
I shall not less thy grace adore,
   So friend forever fare thee well.

Farewell forever did I say?
   What! never more thy face to see?
Then take the last fond look to-day,
   And still to-morrow think of me.

Farewell, alas! the tragic sound,
   Has many a tender bosom torn,
While desolation spread around,
   Deserted friendship left to mourn.

Farewell, awakes the sleeping tear,
   The dormant rill from sorrow's eye,
Expressed from one by nature dear,
   Whose bosom heaves the latent sigh.

Farewell is but departure's tale,
   When fond association ends,
And fate expands her lofty sail,
   to show the distant flight of friends.

Alas! and if we sure must part,
   Far separated long to dwell,
I leave thee with a broken heart,
   So friend forever fare thee well.

I leave thee, but forget thee never,
   Words cannot my feeling tell,
Fare thee well, and if forever,
   Still forever fare thee well.

MY NATIVE HOME

Oh! liberty my native land,
   From thee how can I bear to roam,
Or leave thy patriotic band,
   A stranger to my native home.

The distant isles aspire to thee,
   And plough the ocean's brackish foam,
A land from despotism free,
   My birthright and my native home.

No, let me die upon thy shore,
   And freedom flourish o'er my tomb;
Heaven grant me seraph's wings to soar,
   And leave in peace my native home.

Should I sail to some distant plain,
   Where pleasures laurels fail to bloom,
Oh! fortune o'er the stormy main,
   Back waft me to my native home.

Tho' gold and pearls abundant shine,
   And fortune crown the flowery dome,
But fair Columbia thou art mine,
   The lot of peace my native home.

When smoke from mortars vein the sky,
   With thunders from the shattering bomb,
Oh! let me then with safety fly,
   For shelter to my native home.

Let this be chased in my breast,
   Through this and future years to come,
My last abode, my final rest,
   Be lodged with thee, my native home.

EXECUTION OF PRIVATE HENRY ANDERSON,

Co. D., 9th Mich. Cav. Vols., at Lexington,
North Carolina, May 13th, 1865

This verse is plain, that all may understand,
The scene is solemn and expressly grand;
The must'ring concourse form'd in grand array,
Betrayed the fate of the expiring day;
Gazing spectators seemed completely dumb,
Beneath the sound of bugle and the drum.

The fun'ral march attracted every eye,
To see the trembling malefactor die;
O, memorable even, not soon forgot,
'Tis written on a tablet ne'er to blot;
We never can the scene portray,
The ghastly aspect of the fatal day.

We've heard of martyrs at the cruel stake,
From which an adamantine heart would break;
We've heard of victims on the fun'ral pyre,
Containing sacrifice and set on fire,
When victims died beneath the ruthless flame,
The brutal torture of eternal shame.

This seems to bear the mark, tho' justly done,
A case that every sober man may shun;
'Twas for the deed of open homicide,
This guilty malefactor fell and died.
See well arrayed the attentive squadrons stand,
Thus to discharge their guns at one command;
'Till pointing at one mark the shaft of death,
He breaths at once his last decisive breath.

It is, indeed, a sad infernal crime
To one's own self, thus hurried out of time;
He introduces first the murderous strife,
By his own hand he spurns away his life!
How many creatures thus have fell,
Imbibing nectar from the bowls of hell!

Inspiring depredations all the night,
And thus betrayed the death at morning light;
Thus flies the deadly shaft without control—
He fell upon his coffin, O, my soul!
Let all that live the scene appall—
He dies! no more to live at all, at all!

THE UNION OF PARTIES

Like rivers in conflux, let parties now blend,
Who e'er was a foe, let him now be a friend;
In one tide of glory, together all mix,
The system of concord completely to fix;
    Let us all meet together, and all sing together—
                    In the Union.

Like the union of heaven, the moon and the sun,
At times meet together, a short race to run;
Let us all run together, but not to divide,
That one in the other may safely confide;
    Let us all come together, and all sing together—
                    In the Union.

Meet the lamb and the dove at the national bar,
No thunder of faction their system shall jar;
Like bright constellation in cluster to shine,
Fill the last crash of nature to flow and refine;
    Let us all walk together, and all sing together—
                    In the Union.

We'll mingle in wedlock, we'll mingle in prayer,
To interdict marriage what mortal shall dare;
No longer divided the nation shall be,
Let all go together, by land and by sea;
    Let us all go together, and all stick together—
                    In the Union.

How sweet is the union in heaven we see,
The planets in ether unwavering we see;
In this concentration, harmonious they move,
In wonderful concord, the union of love;
    Then we'll all walk together, and all sing together—
                    In the Union.

LIBERTY

O, Liberty, thou dove of peace,
  We must aspire to thee,
Whose wings thy pinions must release,
  And fan Columbia free.

The torpid reptile in the dust,
  Moves active from thy glee,
And owns the declamation just,
  That nations should be free.

Ye distant isles espouse the theme,
  Far, far, beyond the sea;
The sun declares in every beam,
  All nations should be free.

Hence, let Brittania rage no more,
  Distressing vapors flee,
And bear the news from shore to shore,
  Columbia, still be free.

Editor's note: Printed as "Ode to Liberty" in *Southern Literary Messenger*, April, 1843.

THE ART OF A POET

True nature first inspires the man,
But he must after learn to scan,
    And mark well every rule;
Gradual the climax then ascend,
And prove the contrast in the end,
    Between the wit and fool.

A fool tho' blind, may write a verse,
And seem from folly to emerge,
    And rhyme well every line;
One lucky, void of light, may guess,
And safely to the point may press,
    But this does not refine.

Polish mirror, clear to shine,
And streams must run if they refine,
    And widen as they flow;
The diamonds water lies concealed,
Till polished it is ne'er revealed,
    Its glory bright to show.

A bard must traverse o'er the world,
Where things concealed must rise unfurled,
    And tread the foot of yore;
Tho' he may sweetly harp and sing,
But strictly prune the mental wing,
    Before the mind can soar.

THE HORSE STOLEN FROM THE CAMP

He's gone, alas! I know not whither,
With hair and bones and flesh together;
By hungry fowls he may be slain,
Hence, he will not come back again.

He's gone, but who can show his rider?
Or if concealed, who knows his hider?
One thing is sure, his tramps are o'er,
And hence, will here come back no more!

He's gone, and may be far the better,
As well as mine, the devil's debtor;
He's gone, the buzzard's to deprive,
Who could not take the beast alive.

He's gone, but left no trace behind him,
And hence it will be hard to find him;
If thee no more I'll ride old friend,
My good old pony, fare-thee-well!

ROSABELLA — PURITY OF HEART

Though with an angel's tongue,
  I set on fire the congregations all,
'Tis but a brazen bell that I have rung,
  And I to nothing fall;
My theme is but an idle air,
If Rosabella is not there.

Though I in thunders rave,
  And hurl the blaze of oratoric flowers,
Others I move but fail myself to save,
  With my declaiming powers;
I sink, alas! I know not where,
If Rosabella is not there.

Though I point out the way,
  And closely circumscribe the path to Heaven,
And pour my melting prayer without delay,
  And vow my sins forgiven,
I sink into the gloom, despair,
If Rosabella is not there.

Though I may mountains move,
  And make the valleys vocal with my song,
I'm vain without a stream of mystic love,
  For all my heart is wrong;
I've laid myself a cruel snare,
If Rosabella is not there.

From bibliothic stores
  I fly proclaiming Heaven from land to land,
Or cross the seas and reach their distant shores,
  'Mid gothic groups to stand;
O, let me of myself beware,
If Rosabella is not there.

Our classic books mùst fail,
And with their flow'ry tongue's to ashes burn,
And not one groat a mortal wit avail,
Upon his last return;
Be this the creature's faithful prayer,
That Rosabella may be there.

This spotless maid was born,
The babe of Heaven and cannot be defiled;
The soul is dead and in a state forlorn,
On which she has not smiled;
Vain are the virile and the fair,
If Rosabella be not there.

When other pleasures tire,
And mortal glories fade to glow no more,
She with the wing of truth augments her fire,
And still prevails to soar;
All else must die the good and wise,
But Rosabella never dies.

Editor's note: The poem seems to be a gloss on the First Epistle of Paul to the Corinthians (1 Cor. 13:1, 2, 8–13), which begins, "Though I speak with the tongues of men and of angels, and have not charity, I am become as sounding brass, or a tinkling cymbal." Horton replaces "charity" with "purity of heart."

SLAVERY

Slavery, thou peace-disturbing thief,
  We can't but look with frowns on thee,
Without the balm which gives relief,
  The balm of birthright—Liberty.

Thy wing has been for ages furl'd,
  Thy vessel toss'd from wave to wave,
By stormy winds 'mid billows hurl'd—
  Such is the fate of every slave.

A loathesome burden we are to bear,
  Through sultry bogs we trudging go;
Thy rusty chains we frown to wear,
  Without one inch of wealth to show.

Our fathers from their native land
  Were dragged across the brackish deep,
Bound fast together, hand in hand,
  O! did the God of nature sleep?

When sadly thro' the almond grove
  The pirate dragged them o'er the sod,
Devoid of pity and of love,
  They seemed as left without a God.

Are we not men as well as they,
  Born to enjoy the good of earth,
Brought in creation from the clay,
  To reap a blessing from our birth?

Alas! how can such rebels thrive,
  Who take our lives and wealth away,
Since all were placed on earth to live,
  And prosper by the light of day.

The maledictions of our God,
  Pervade the dwindling world we see;
He hurls the vengeance with his rod,
  And thunders, let the slave be free!

TO THE MUSE

Dear muse, to thee I lift mine eyes,
　And supplicate thy power;
Tho' at thy feet a suppliant lie,
And heaves his penitential sigh,
　To thy exalted tower.

Gladly I move at thy behest,
　Thou garden of my mind;
Distant from thee I cannot rest,
But where thou art, my heart is blest,
　And all to thee resigned.

Not one that shines among the fair
　Delights me dear like thee,
For when the vapors of despair
Assail my heart, if thou art there
　I crave not else to see.

When lightning blazes o'er my head,
　Thy smiles my duty form;
The sun of hope beyond the dead,
Why should that soul the thunder dread,
　Or fear to meet the storm.

When mortal life is almost gone,
　Thou beck'nest from the tomb,
The veil will shortly be withdrawn,
The smiles of an ethereal dawn
　Will swallow nature's gloom.

When fleshly powers decline to sing,
　And love deserts its claim,
My soul tune every dulcet string,
Till my dear muse upon the wing,
　Escorts thee safe away.

THE INTEMPERANCE CLUB

On smiling wealth, intemp'rance war began,
  Away young health and mother genius flew;
And when from [health] the child and parent ran,
  In stepped Dyspepsia belching, how do ye do?

'Twas then the din of desperation rose,
  Pleasure and pain at once their daggers drew;
Pain with his rod struck pleasure on the nose—
  In stepped lean Palsy trembling, how do ye do?

Young health came back to take a peep,
  But stay'd not long the ghastly sight to view;
And on her flight could not forbear to weep—
  In stepped the Cholic frowning, how do ye do?

She heard the crash of gambling rend the floor,
  And in the house saw poverty's dull crew;
When down the foot of Bolus kicked the door—
  In stepped the King of Terrors, how do ye do?

SNAPS FOR DINNER, SNAPS FOR BREAKFAST AND SNAPS FOR SUPPER

Come in to dinner, squalls the dame,
    You need it now perhaps;
But hear the husband's loud exclaim,
    I do not like your snaps;
'Tis snaps when at your breakfast meal,
    And snaps when at your spinning wheel,
Too many by a devilish deal,
    For all your words are snaps.

Why do you tarry, tell me why?
    The chamber door she taps;
Eat by yourself, my dear, for I
    Am surfeited with snaps;
For if I cough it is the cry,
    You always snap at supper time,
I'd rather lave in vats of lime,
    Than face you with your snaps.

How gladly would I be a book,
    To your long pocket flaps,
That you my face may read and look,
And learn the worth of snaps;
I'm sorry that I learning lack
    To turn you to an almanac;
Next year I'll hang you on the rack,
    And end the date of snaps.

THE OBSTRUCTION OF GENIUS

I am surveyed by envy's eye,
   By white and colored all the same,
Which oft draws out a secret sigh,
   To feel the ills that bother fame.

Throughout my life I've tried the path,
   Which seemed as leading out of gloom,
Beneath my feet still kindled wrath,
   Genius seemed leading to a tomb.

No cultivating hand was found,
   To urge the night improving shave,
Never by freedom's laurel crowned,
   But pushed through hardship to the grave.

Has philanthropic vigor slept,
   So long in cells of disregard,
While genius in his fetters wept,
   Devoid of favors or reward.

They often fly to trivial pleas,
   To interdict the important cause,
To crush the negligent disease,
   And kill the force of humane laws.

Why did the Gods of Afric sleep,
   Forgetful of their guardian love,
When the white traitors of the deep
   Betray'd him in the palmy grove.

Let us the evil now forget,
   Which darkened the Columbian shore,
Till sun shall fail to rise and set,
   And slavery's cries are heard no more.

Acrostics, 61
Art of a Poet, The, 147
Cheerless Condition of Bachelorship, The, 128
Close of Life, The, 137
Connubial Felicity, 111
Creditor to His Proud Debtor, The, 96
Death of an Old Carriage Horse, 136
Division of an Estate, 100
Early Affection, 104
Excited from Reading the Obedience of Nature to Her Lord in the Vessel on the Sea, 55
Execution of Private Henry Anderson . . ., 143
Farewell to Frances, 141
Fate of an Innocent Dog, The, 106
Fearful Traveller in the Haunted Castle, The, 114
For the fair Miss M. M. McL[ean], 64
Gen. Grant—The Hero of the War, 122
George Moses Horton, Myself, 121
Graduate Leaving College, The, 103
Gratitude, 58
Heavenly Love, 86
Horse Stolen from the Camp, The, 148
Imploring to be Resigned at Death, 102
Intemperance Club, The, 154
Jefferson in a Tight Place, 125
Liberty, 146
Lincoln is Dead, 127
Lines, On hearing . . ., 90
Lines to My ——, 60
Love, 78
Man, A Torch, 118
Meditation on a Cold, Dark and Rainy Night, 113
My Native Home, 142
New Fashions, 132
Obstruction of Genius, The, 156
On an Old Deluded Suitor, 95
One Generation Passeth Away and Another Cometh, 133
On Liberty and Slavery, 75
On Summer, 82
On the Evening and Morning, 87
On the Pleasures of College Life, 108
On the Poetic Muse, 89

On the Truth of the Saviour, 80
On Winter, 84
Poet's Feeble Petition, The, 62
Praise of Creation, 73
Reflections from the Flash of a Meteor, 105
Retreat from Moscow, The, 98
Rosabella—Purity of Heart, 149
Slave, The, 130
Slavery (1828), 56
Slavery (1865), 151
Slave's Complaint, The, 79
Slave's Reflections the Eve Before His Sale, 139
Snaps for Dinner, Snaps for Breakfast and Snaps for Supper, 155
Song of Liberty and Parental Advice, 134
Southern Refugee, The, 124
Tippler to His Bottle, The, 112
To Eliza, 77
To the Muse, 153
Troubled with the Itch, and Rubbing with Sulphur, 116
Union of Parties, The, 145
Woodman and Money Hunter, The, 117